Blood on

Uncovering the Assault Sites of my Toddlerhood

Madeleine Watson

Madeleine Watson

To Sam

Contents

Introduction   3

1   **The Journey Begins**   7

Map of Raventree and
Surrounding Villages   10

2   **Jaunts Instigated by Others**   12

3   **Jaunts Instigated by Me**   34

4   **Jaunts and Boyfriends**   73

5   **Driving Lessons**   76

6   **Conclusion**   79

Other Books by the Author   80

Introduction

The following story is true.

On 26 October 2016, a horrific memory surfaced. I was fifty-one years old and gleaning through one of my novels. I had begun to realise my novels weren't what I thought they were and I was asking questions about my past. I have been writing stories since I was about six and producing copious artwork too. I spent five years at art school and by the age of twenty-one, had attained a Fine Art degree. Creativity runs in the family and I thought nothing of it. But at times, mine runs into another realm. I would get odd notions and a project would take a hold on me. Often I would keep my diversions secret from family and friends.

What I didn't realise was that clues to my horrific toddlerhood were leaking into my creations.

Yes, my toddlerhood.

I have come to learn I was raped at the age of three.

Something Wrong

Throughout my life, I felt something was wrong with me. At infant school a school psychologist was called in for my disruptive behaviour. I couldn't bond in groups and would retreat into a shell. I often zoned-out in class, losing track of what was going on and struggled with comprehension. Worst of all, I suffered inexplicable intrusive thoughts – things like a face ablaze in a cave to ominous drumbeats and falling into a coma. I got this notion of bodies walled up or catatonic in beds. This vile imagery made no sense and I couldn't bear to contemplate where they came, nor even acknowledge their existence. Gradually, I got this strange notion of something to the northeast of me. It wasn't horrible. In fact, this presence reassured. I wanted to go over there but I didn't know what it was or where this place was. Inexplicable grief would crash into me without warning and I'd feel like crying for no apparent reason.

When I was eleven, Mum took me to the doctors for depression. For years, I had avoided my bed and kept wanting the lights on. Without knowing what was wrong with me, the doctor could only conclude I was suffering routine night terrors and that I would grow out of them.

His words gave comfort. Perhaps he was right. I live in a rundown cottage with four siblings at the time, including my identical twin, Eve. The place was old with shadowy corners and creaky floorboards. Small wonder a young child with a feverish imagination would get unsettling notions. Dad was mentally ill, too. He'd been out of work since I was four after suffering a nervous breakdown. He was prescribed all sorts of anti-

3

psychotics to curb his tempers. My parents had an appalling marriage and bad atmospheres were the norm. A few times, he'd come out of nowhere and vent his rage if I happened to be in the wrong place at the wrong time. At his worst, he terrified me.

And so I attributed my problems to this.

Nothing but this.

Rendered invisible was my uncle's stay at the cottage throughout my toddlerhood.

The Truth Hidden

Mum's half-brother, Uncle Dan, lived with us for most of 1968. He slept in a guestroom to the north of the cottage. His stay was seldom mentioned and I kept gleaning over this detail, assuming he had nothing to do with me whatsoever. He was forty-seven at the time, so why should he? A mechanism in my head kept making small of it. He 'stopped briefly' or 'not at all'. Uncle Dan was in the Metropolitan Police for ten years. He served time in the army, prison and a mental hospital. He had travelled the world, got into trouble and had affairs. His gallivanting reinforced the notion he was a distant uncle and that he lived far away – far, far away from me. In fact, he lived in my childhood cottage throughout the third year of my life and I had failed to grasp the implications.

For sensitive reasons, I have changed his name and I am writing under a pseudonym.

The Memory

The memory was of being suffocated by Uncle Dan.

One cloudy afternoon, he entered my bedroom half-stripped and mounted my bed. He sat on my chest and grunting something. Not understanding, I complied. He then locked my head between his legs and applied such pressure, my face felt ablaze. Within seconds, I blacked out before rousing with something horrible on my face. Being only three, I didn't understand the concept of abuse. He was like a parent-figure and I assumed he was doing something as his right. My intrusive thoughts of a face ablaze within caves now make sense. I was suffering flashbacks to being suffocated and orally raped by Uncle Dan.

When the horrific memory came up, the life I had believed in was destroyed. I didn't know who I was anymore and the family I grew up with suddenly seemed like strangers. To exacerbate matters, Mum passed away six weeks after I had seen this memory. As she had been ill for over a year by then, I never got the chance to tell her what her half-brother had done to me. Uncle Dan had been dead sixteen years by then.

4

For months afterwards, my life fell apart, while everything carried on as normal. I had worked hard to get where I am today. I live with my partner, Paul and two children in a semi, and I worked in Land Law and Education. Somehow, I have to continue being a mum and partner; somehow I have to continue being the person I believed I was. Meanwhile, a part of me is slowly dying. I cannot look upon the past in the same way again.

Since the horrific memory surfaced, I have discovered clues to my toddlerhood stowed within my creations. Double-meaning and hidden plotlines are encoded in my stories; symbolism in my art. These clues don't feel mine. It's as though someone else had put them there, not me and I am trying to understand what these clues are.

False Belief

This book has been written four years after I had seen that horrific memory, and my creations continue to give up secrets. I have come to realise the devastation my toddlerhood has had upon my life. It is truly monstrous and yet I saw none of it at all.

I have lived for almost fifty years under the firm belief I have never been sexually abused whatsoever. In fact, my appalling toddlerhood has leached into areas of my life beyond comprehension.

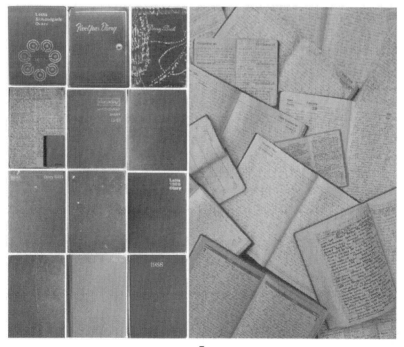

5

The previous images show my diaries of eleven-and-a-half years. The image on the right shows my copious entries within. As can be seen, my recordkeeping was quite extensive.

My Diaries

To date, I have analysed my children's stories, my novels and artwork. The process has been intensive and harrowing. I am now analysing my diaries.

Between 1977 and 1988, I kept a detailed one. In the Eighties, I reported on all sorts of things from the weather to my moods. Little did I realise, the effects of my toddlerhood are being recorded too. All would remain invisible along with the truth.

In later years, I would keep a small works diary where the aftershocks of my toddlerhood are still going strong. My diaries have been vital to my research but there is a lot of data to get through. Where do I begin?

I decide to assign categories, things like my tastes in films and books, my hobbies, my projects, my children's stories, doll-playing, guitar songs, quizzes and others. And then there's my jogging, my swimming, my brief smoking-habit, my relationships, my jobs, my marriage and more. And not least, is my disturbed nights, health niggles, mood swings and depression. Every strand interconnects to others in a complex tapestry. The big picture is unequivocal. How hadn't I seen it?

The Jaunts

To this day, Dad remains oblivious to what I have discovered about Uncle Dan. Dad is now in his eighties and I feel loathe to ask about his brother-in-law. Dad's answers could cause further distress and I couldn't risk a sour farewell anon. The same goes for my siblings. Instead, I made a statement to the police and do my research alone.

This book examines one strand in particular: jaunts to the east of the village. This strand has divulged of assault sites. Uncle Dan took Eve and me out in our double pushchair and committed acts of rape on deserted roadsides.

This book explains how I have worked out where these sites are. My bike rides and walks to a region outside of the village has left clues. My twin, Eve and (occasionally) other family members came on these jaunts too. My diary reports of dates, routes, the weather, my mood and behaviour at the time. My oblivion to Uncle Dan's presence in my toddlerhood was complete, yet vital to finding the truth.

My journey into the past starts here.

1. The Journey Begins

Eve is my identical twin. In our early years, we were always together. I have therefore witnessed things and she has witnessed things too. But like me, she has remained oblivious to her toddlerhood and blamed her problems upon the wrong things. Sadly, it was me that told her what I have discovered and this has caused memories of her own to surface. I have come to learn Uncle Dan vaginally raped me, but not Eve. I believed he stuck to the same twin after I had lost blood in order to avoid leaving unnecessary clues and the likelihood of getting caught.

Dad told me he used to let Uncle Dan take Eve and me out in our double pushchair. Indeed, I have a memory of a dark-haired man ferrying Eve and me across recreation grounds to a small thicket called Privy Woods. I feel nothing when I think of this memory, nothing at all. This void-feeling has caused this memory to recede into the background. I would therefore claim to have no memory of Uncle Dan whatsoever. In fact I have several memories of Uncle Dan and all these memories have been pushed into the background in just the same way.

I have since learned that trauma memories are fragmented, which explains why I feel nothing when I think of this memory. The trauma aspect has been stored separately in the brain and emerge in the form of flashbacks and intrusive thoughts that make no sense. For decades, I had failed to see what these visions were and that they belong to these early memories.

The Responses

My behaviour towards various sites of my childhood village in later years are revealing. Despite being at the heart (and providing a convenient short-cut to junior school), I barely stepped foot in Privy Woods. I was avoiding these woods without realising what I was doing. This is because Uncle Dan raped me in those woods when I was a toddler and I was avoiding it in subsequent years. Places I didn't know existed burned in my head, like wheatfields and clearings, railway tracks and a sunburst lane forever going eastwards.

Uncle Dan lived with us for over a year and Privy Woods isn't the only rape site. He raped me in other locations of the village too.

After carefully researching my diaries, I have been able to establish these assault sites. My subconscious knows the locations, and exposure to these places has triggered a response. These responses are reported in my diaries but remained unrecognised until now. I didn't know the truth about myself and had explained these responses to something else.

The photos show landmarks of my childhood village.

Top row (from left): The disused railway station, now privately owned. Raventree church, a big part of my childhood.

Middle row: Privy Woods from the recreation grounds, now (mostly) built over. Accessway between Privy Woods, the church and my school.

Bottom row: The Inn and Weavers pubs cornering Fox Road that leads eastwards out of the village.

The Disused Railway Station

A chief assault site was at the foot of a disused railway station to the west of the village. This station has been out of use since 1933 and is accessed by a little lane on the roadside.

Whenever I traversed this railway station on my way to senior school, notions of a big man standing beside the railway track started to invade my head. I would eventually write about him in my first novel called *The Lessons*. I had believed this novel routine fiction and I was a routine author. In fact, this novel would soon take a grip on my life because my horrific toddlerhood was fuelling it. The result would be that clues to the rape are stowed within what appears to be a staple thriller. I learned of the disused railway station through this novel, not my jaunts. The story is complex and doesn't feel right here.

Excluding my childhood cottage, I have uncovered five assault sites. Privy Woods and the disused railway station have been explained. But what about the other three? Had it not been for my abundant creations, I wouldn't have known about any of these sites, let alone Uncle Dan.

What my Diaries Tell Me

The records given here are as accurate as I can make them. I have closely examined my diaries and have come to learn an incredible amount about my toddlerhood.

Throughout the Seventies, my childhood village was surrounded with countryside. Naturally, I went for walks and bike rides to various locations. From the late Seventies to the early Eighties, Eve and I ventured out. At the beginning, Dad instigated our jaunts, as we were mere schoolgirls at the time. He would spruce up old bikes salvaged from the tip and (when he was well) took us on these jaunts. My bike had only one gear and hills were strenuous. Still, I loved that bike, having known no different.

From 8th July 1981, Eve and I went on these bike rides on our own. I would instigate these rides and plan the routes. Otherwise, we would walk. These jaunts were often to the east of the village. This is because quiet country lanes and pretty villages can be found there. Since learning the truth about my toddlerhood, I have uncovered troubling patterns in my behaviour around these jaunts. This is because (without my conscious awareness) I was encountering rape sites of my toddlerhood.

Map of Raventree and Surrounding Villages

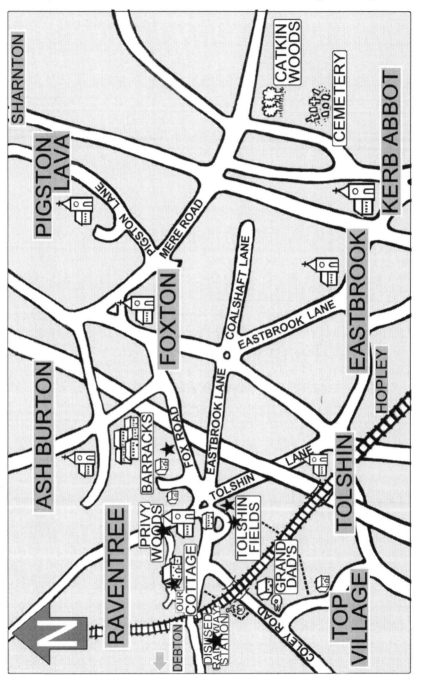

The map shows the village of Raventree, location of my childhood cottage. Raventree is an assumed name, but the geography is exactly the same as the place where I grew up. Also shown are the surrounding villages where I took these bike rides and walks. A railway track cuts to the southwest of the village and a motorway slices northwards. The small town of Debton is accessed by going over the disused railway station to the west.

Worth noting, is Granddad's who lived on Coley Road near the railway track. A couple of footpaths cut beneath the railway line across fields on either side of his house. One of these leads to Top Village, just a mile or so away.

Several further villages dot the countryside to the east. These are Foxton, Eastbrook, Hopley, Tolshin, Kerb Abbot, Pigston Lava and Ash Burton. Army barracks stand between Ash Burton and Raventree. Like Raventree, most of these villages have their own church.

The black stars mark assault sites established, including Privy Woods (short for 'Private Woods') and the disused railway station. The cottage where I lived of course is another. The three remaining sites are a farmer's gate on Fox Road, scrublands overlooking Tolshin Fields and the edge of Tolshin Lane.

In order to protect my identity, I have altered placenames, but strong parallels exist with the real ones.

Retracing the Past

Since learning about my appalling toddlerhood, I have retraced these bike rides and walks. Almost four decades have elapsed since I had been to some of these places and the cottage had sold in 1996. I no longer have much to do with Raventree and yet once upon a time, it had been the centre of my existence.

In September 2020, I loaned a bike, drove to the village and entered the past. Only by these means can I experience these roads as the diarist I once was. Only then can I be certain I haven't missed anything.

The experience has been poignant but has opened my eyes. Why did these trips leave me feeling sad and unsettled? The weather is lovely, the villages scenic. And yet something was wrong, very wrong.

This book describes how I have come to learn where a part of me has been lost.

2. Jaunts Instigated by Others
(30 April 1977 – 8 July 1981)

In the early days, Mum or Dad instigated our jaunts. This was natural as Eve and I were schoolgirls at the beginning. Until then, I had not encountered these assault sites (except in the car) since toddlerhood. As these trips weren't instigated by myself, cannot be seen as being of my actions. I am therefore encountering an assault site due to someone else and I would be 'triggered'. A response of some kind will come about, which could be depression, health niggles or a particular behaviour.

As will be seen.

JAUNTS OF 1977

My first diary was small and little room was permitted on each page to write much, so details are sketchy here. However, this is what I have found.

30 April 1977: Mystery at Hornfield

My first report of going on a bike ride was 30 April 1977. Dad took Eve and me to Granddad's who lived on Coley Road. This bike ride happened to occur within an existing episode spurred by another trigger. The day previously, a neighbourhood boy kept flashing at us from his bedroom window. Two days later, I am writing a haunting children's story called *Mystery at Hornfield*. Like my novels, my children's mysteries inform upon my toddlerhood. So the sight of a penis had triggered my writing.

28 July 1977: A Twenty-Mile Bike Ride

Three months later, Dad took Eve and me on a bike ride twenty miles out. I know this to be the east of the village but my diary doesn't say exactly where. Still, I had likely encountered the Fox Road assault site.

The following day, I walked to Granddads. A few days later, I'm crying. No reason is given but I clearly recall this bike ride and felt unsettled, wrong. I didn't know why.

30 Dec 1977: A Walk in the Snow

This is the third bike ride of 1977. I am feeling bored and restless over the Christmas holidays so Dad takes Eve and me for a four-mile walk in the snow. My diary doesn't say where, but I believe it was across Tolshin Fields, leading to Top Village. On the 31st, I would go on this four-mile walk alone. This seems odd, as I was twelve at the time and was often with my twin. I report of feeling sad during the walk. Early in the New Year, I'm messing a lot with a toy guitar I'd had for Christmas.

My solo walk appears to be a response to a trigger: a walk Dad had taken me the day previously.

So far, little can be seen from this, until looking at my later diaries.

JAUNTS OF 1978

In 1978, I had two diaries. Between them, there is more room to report things like bike routes and my mood. One of them is a five-year diary, the other is a stand-alone diary. Sometimes, I would repeat myself in each one; at other times, I would write something only in one of them.

I am now describing the routes in my diaries. For clarity, I have supplied a map for each route given. The map shows the previous map faded out. The cottage remains bold, as well as assault sites (shown as black stars.) Highlighted are routes from the cottage. Where no route is described in my diary, no map is provided.

As can be seen, a bigger story stitches together these bike rides.

ROUTE 1: **18 July 1978: The Skull and Broken Guitar**

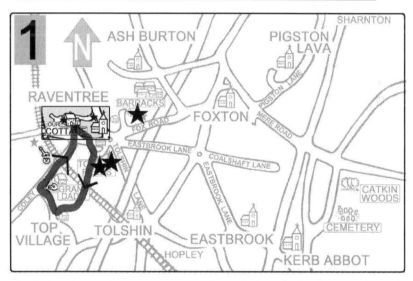

Dad, Eve, Mazie (my youngest sister), Nicholas (my brother) and I walk across Tolshin Fields to a pub in Top Village. We return via Granddad's on Coley Road.

Images: Granddad's bungalow on Coley Road, the railway bridge nearby, the broken guitar (recreated) and the brook where the skull was found.

The day starts bad and I feel bored. Dad takes Eve, my brother Nicholas, my youngest sister Mazie and me for a walk across Tolshin Fields. We stop at a pub in Top Village for shandy and crisps. We then round off our walk by stopping at Granddad's. The following day, We visit Granddad's again to find his sisters there. I am feeling very depressed. I have established the scrublands of Tolshin Fields to be an assault site and we had just cut through it.

To complicate matters, the previous April, I had found an animal skull in a brook near Granddad's. A few days after this find, I would encounter a tramp's hut, torn cheques, a broken guitar and bikes on the railway track nearby. These finds had spurred subconscious notions of head trauma, a broken self and an exile. (The bike and guitar were like 'mine' and a part of me has been banished into no-man's land). A huge writing episode had then resulted. Granddad's has now become tarnished with notions of toddlerhood traumas because of these objects. In thirty-two years' time, I would write a novel, *North Window* about a broken guitar and a malevolent force. The broken finds of 1978 had been wiped from my conscious awareness at the time of writing this novel.

A Mock Assault Site

So Granddad's road has become like an assault site, even though it isn't. Coley Road is too open to commit a criminal act. I do not believe Uncle Dan took me there. In future years, further 'mock assault' sites will be created due to encounters, and responses will come about. The skull and broken guitar are shown bold to the left of the map.

The day after visiting Granddad's (and soon after walking over Tolshin Fields), I'm 'writing in my folder all day.' This folder contains my stories. I make up a game called Lucky Chart and I have a new string on my guitar for making up songs. I can't sleep that night and come down with a bad headache and stiff joints. I end up taking painkillers and bedding early. I believe these symptoms were triggered by encountering an assault site and a 'mock' assault site.

As will be seen, my obsessive hobbying and illnesses appear to time-in with such encounters on these jaunts. These patterns would grow prevalent in future years.

24 July 1978: The Guestroom

Six days after going to Granddad's, Dad takes Eve and me on a long bike ride, which I know begins on Fox Road. No map is supplied here, as my diary doesn't specify the route. We'd had a false start, as Dad's inner tube had exploded soon after we set off and he used Nicolas's bike instead. I had put a plectrum on my wheel so it would make a buzzing sound (a brief craze in the Seventies). I remark we had seen a' rabbit and a horse'. I recall animal pens situated along Fox Road. My tyre goes flat on our return. This bike ride is interesting and offers further insight.

Dad's bedroom used to be Uncle Dan's. It was then known as the guestroom. I have come to learn, I was raped in that room. The day after this bike ride, I go 'secretly' to Dad's bedroom.

The next day, I would repeat this behaviour, going 'secretly to Dad's bedroom'. This time, I look in the family bible and in a 'hiding place'. To my subconscious, this bible symbolized the deep past – mine. The meaning of this is toddlerhood. And what of this 'hiding place?' Strangely, these secret visits to Dad's bedroom were reported *only* in my five-year diary, not the standalone one. It's like a half-disclosure where my standalone diary represents my oblivion.

15

The Big Use of my Toddlerhood

On 30th July 1979, I would hide a blonde-haired doll called Big Sue in this same hiding place of Dad's bedroom. I now realise Sue was an effigy of my toddlerhood self and her name is an anagram of 'big use', for this was how I felt in toddlerhood: used. Encodings like these will occur in other proper nouns of my stories. All Sue did was lay apparently asleep in my pantos while the other toys ran amok. Little did I realise she is roleplaying my comatose self in post assault.

In the summer of 1980, I would make toys for Mazie and stow then in the same hiding place of Dad's bedroom. I was suffering a bad cough at the time. My throat forms a trauma site which seems to be activated by toddlerhood mementoes. Again, this bike ride appears to have triggered me into visiting a rape site in the cottage, checking out a 'hiding place' of Big Sue and the family bible that delves into the deep past.

See how these bike rides are triggering me? This is because I am encountering rape sites of my toddlerhood without my conscious awareness.

ROUTE 2: **29 July 1978: Pig's ton Lava and the Land of Berks**

Dad, Eve and I cycle to Pigston Lava, stopping at Kerb Abbot. We cut through Tolshin, Hopley and Top Village, returning via Granddad's on Coley Road.

On 29th July 1978, Dad takes Eve and me on a bike ride all morning beginning with Fox Road. We encounter the oddly-named villages of Pigston Lava and Kerb Abbot.

On our return, we stopped at Top Village for shandy and crisps (we had been to this pub on the 18th of July). Eve had bike trouble and Dad nicked some oil from a barn to fix it. Later that day, I played swing-ball with a girl called June Cox who lived over the fence from us. Her Dad bore a vague semblance to Uncle Dan for being tall, dark and moustached. Visits to her house has shown to trigger symptoms and behaviour within me.

The following day, I report of rousing early to rain. I'm already unsettled. Cousin Matt from Canada visits and I played badminton with him. (In August, Matt would sleep in Dad's room, causing further triggers). I play a guitar song to Granddad and his sister who also visited that day. I would then begin a story, *Green Croft*.

Pig's-ton-Lava, the Village Abandoned

Since learning about my toddlerhood, I have discovered I have a plural. This plural is like a version of me who knows everything about my toddlerhood while 'I' know nothing. Her toxic knowledge has been quarantined off to protect my mind. But this doesn't stop this exiled part of me from making associations with my toddlerhood traumas and the after scars. Included is how she perceives road names and landmarks. Pigston Lava, for instance (to her) means pig (slang for policeman, as was Uncle Dan) 'on' (or ton, as he was heavy) 'lava', meaning me, burning under his immense pressure during assault. What a bizarre thing. It's as though this village name was waiting for me.

My visits to Pigston Lava is always a village deserted. it's like a ghost village. I have encountered a lawn with fallen apples (like my childhood lawn); leaded windows (like those of my childhood cottage) and a concealed church. It's like an alternative Raventree, an abandoned Raventree of her memories, all because of the 'Pigston Lava'. No wonder I wouldn't return to this village for almost forty years.

Berk-Kerb and Oblivion

Our next stop is Kerb Abbot.

Kerb Abbot has a disproportionally large church. It dominates the skyline. I have come to learn that (to my plural) church has become a symbol of the born-again virgin, for associations with decency and purity. Church was a big part of my childhood, as Mum enforced upon me

17

Sunday attendance and other involvements. In the mid-Seventies, I clung to church through fear. I used to write prayers.

On decoding my stories and novels, I have uncovered an under-language. A fictional place called Berkham recurs in my novels. The hidden meaning of this is 'am berk'. Being a berk. In other words, dumb, oblivious. The reverse spelling of berk is 'kerb'. In my final novel, *Nadia*, kerbing was blamed for a car crash, that wasn't really a crash at all, but assault. It's a cover-up. This berk-kerb thing means being a berk and going with my assumed childhood virginity. It all goes back to Kerb Abbot with the huge church.

The Cemetery, Catkin Woods and Privy Woods

Just outside Kerb Abbot stands a cemetery. This cemetery is stowed within trees, as though banished from the church. To my plural this 'banished' cemetery has come to represent the burial of my past.

Further up the lane are woods, which I have called Catkin Woods for this account. When I was seven, Dad took Eve and me to these woods via car to pick catkins and pussy willows for school. I had just begun my third year at infants, making this September 1972. The day was cloudy and I recall feeling horribly uneasy within a clearing.

I now realise these woods had reminded me of Privy Woods where I was raped four years earlier, only I couldn't see it. The day after our trip in the car, a zookeeper had visited our classroom with badgers, foxes and birds. Already, I feel different to my classmates and can't seem to forge relationships. The year previously, Eve and I had to see a child psychologist because of our disruptive behaviour.

The landmarks of Kerb Abbot have come to symbolise an overstatement of virginity (the church) and the burial (the cemetery) of my rape in Privy Woods (akin to Catkin Woods).

This bike ride had begun on Fox Road too, an assault site.

My behaviour towards these villages will further illuminate upon how my plural thinks.

*Images left: **Pigston Lava**: The church, a cottage, felled apples on a lawn and a quiet lane. It's like another Raventree, but which is now abandoned. **Images right: Kerb Abbot**: The mighty church and cottages. **Images far right (from top)**: Kerb Abbot's cemetery, Catkin Woods, pussy willows and catkins.*

24 and 26 Sept 1978: A Surge of Stories Through Writing and Pantos

On the 24th of Sept, Dad takes Eve and me on a short bike ride to the east of the village. I don't know where, hence no map. But on the same day, I revive the Secret Amethyst Club with Eve and Nicholas. This club is centred on the upkeep of hobbies – always hobbies. My siblings don't share my fervour because something about me is wrong. I am writing a story (untitled) and I go to June Cox's house on the 25th. On the 26th, I go on a bike ride with Dad to Granddad's where I got very depressed. The following day, I'm playing dolls (starring Big Sue) with Eve and Mazie. (I hadn't played dolls since 27th Aug). My depression, stories, songs and pantos have been triggered by mementos of my toddlerhood.

JAUNTS OF 1979

14 April 1979: A Long Bike Ride and Jigsaws

My first bike ride reported in 1979 is a long one with Dad and Eve. I don't know where we went and little detail is given. This is because I am making do with a small, crappy five-year diary. In fifteen months' time, my diary would make a transformation. For now, the weather is fair and I am doing a lot of jigsaws. Some are a thousand pieces and others I do more than once. Diversions again.

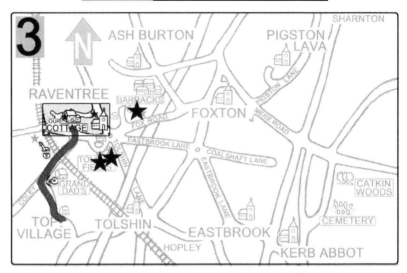

Dad takes Eve and me for a bike ride down Coley Road and Top Village.

Today, I report that Dad takes Eve and me on a bike ride past Granddad's house on our way to Top Village. Sadly, Granddad had died on the 28th of Jan that year. He fell and burnt his face on the fireplace. How terrible. A burnt face resonates with my sensation of immense pressure during suffocation in toddlerhood. This 'mock' assault site has added fuel now.

I had visited Granddad's house for the final time on 21st May before it sells on the 17th July. From here-on, I shall change 'Granddad's to 'Coley Road', for the bungalow is no longer his.

A day after this bike ride, I'm off from school and writing an illustrated story. (I had already written a story on the 17th). I'm feeling unwell and by the 23rd, my ailments gather to a nasty head-cold and headache, but I manage to read my story to Eve and Mazie on the 24th. I then play dolls with the same two sisters. My symptoms are telling on the trauma sites, being the head, throat and vagina. As is often the case, a creative surge has accompanied. The culprit is Coley Road, a mock assault site.

28 Aug 1979: Lost in the Garden

The summer holidays are ending. Dad takes Eve and me on a bike ride to the east of the village. I'm still making do with my crappy five-year diary, which permits little room for detail. Afterwards, I frantically tidy the playhouse and weed the path. I'm doing a lot of gardening and I cry through 'boredom'. In fact, it's depression and I am seeking diversion again. On the 29th, I got a letter from the Meteorological Office. Enclosed is a huge weather map displaying a classic cyclone, complete with spiralling isobars. For years, I have been fascinated with nature's fury such as hurricanes and tornadoes. To my subconscious, looking at this cyclone is like holding a mirror to the trauma in my head. My weather project, like my stories, novels and artwork, is fuelled by my toddlerhood.

On the 30th Aug and the following few days, I am playing dolls (with Big Sue) again. Nan (my uncle's mother) has been stopping with us and on the 1st Sept, she returns to Mum's half-sister, Aunt Maud.

ROUTE 4: **10 June 1979: Sean Linton**

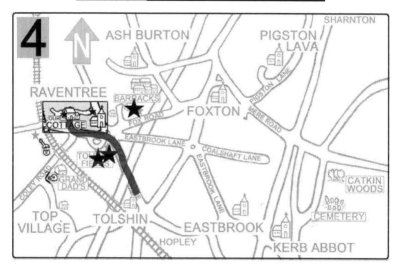

Mum, Eve and I walk down Tolshin Lane.

Mum, Eve and I go on a long walk down Tolshin Lane, not quite reaching the village. Tolshin Lane has proven to be an assault site. A recurring nightmare had told me so: I'm being pursued on a stretch of road which I believed was imaginary. The sky was biblical and something nasty was going to get me. Little did I realise, I was dreaming of a real road and an actual memory. It is Tolshin Lane and something bad *had* happened to me. In 2009 (seven years before recall), I would write a short story called *Deadline*. A character called Sean Linton suffers head trauma. Tolshin Lane is encoded in his name. Notice the 'lane'-anagram connecting the names: S-*eanl*-inton. Sean contains the phonic 'sh' and Linton could have two 'll's (Shean Llinton). The remaining syllables can be rearranged to

21

create 'Tolshin'. This (as well as other reasons) tells me Tolshin Lane is an assault site and I had suffered head trauma there. My creations are fuelled by my appalling toddlerhood and therefore give (disguised) accounts of what happened. Later that day, I'm devising quizzes and playing dolls (starring 'Big Use') with Eve and Mazie.

17 July 1979: Tree Fungus in Top Village

Dad, Eve, Maze and I went on a five-mile walk where Eve found a large brown fungus in Top Village. She is at this time interested in Mycology (the study of mushrooms and toadstools). I feel this diversion (like my fascination with nature's fury) is informing upon something she had seen in woods.

JAUNTS OF 1980

A new decade has now begun. Dad continues to instigate our bike rides. I continue to encounter assault sites of my toddlerhood and responses continue to occur. My 1980 diary is small, just like my 1979 one. Again, little room is permitted on each page. But on 20th of July 1980, I would begin a large diary. I would soon dedicate an A4 sheet to every day, reporting on what I wore, ate, the weather and more. I feel this transformation is the doing of my plural. She wants disclosure and dreams that one day I will do this research with her.

ROUTE 5: 11 May 1980: Brewer Road

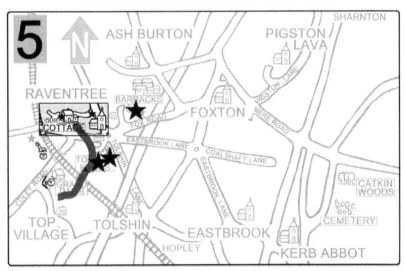

Dad takes Eve and me for a walk across Tolshin Fields

Dad takes Eve and me for a long trek over Tolshin Fields. We walk under a railway bridge to reach Top Village, before returning via the same route. Scrublands and allotments abut these fields. I was assaulted in those scrublands.

A road called Brewer Road stands near these scrublands. The name Brewer repeats in my stories without any conscious knowledge of this road at all. Brewer brings fear and aversion in my fictional characters.

Top row (from left): Two assault sites close together: Tolshin Lane and scrublands abutting Tolshin Fields.
Middle row: The complex where Nan (my uncle's mother) lived in 1986-7. It is close to these assault sites. A view of Tolshin Fields from the scrublands.
Bottom row: Railway tunnel cutting through Tolshin Fields towards Top Village. A lane leading out of Top Village.

Brewer Road and Scrublands

I would write about scrublands and allotments overlooking fields in *Outside* (2012) a short story about assault (disguised as something else). It's just like my other short story, *Deadline* with Sean Linton. All my stories are fuelled by my toddlerhood and tell me things outside of my conscious awareness. I had believed these scrublands fictional, yet both sites are close to Brewer Road. This road may have formed a route to these assault sites.

Six years would pass before I'd set eyes upon Tolshin Fields again and a further six before I'd traverse them. Like with Privy Woods, I was avoiding a place without realising what I was doing. Since recall occurred in 2016, I have walked across Tolshin Fields, and strong emotional and physical responses have resulted.

As can be seen from the map, two assault sites huddle up: Tolshin Lane and Tolshin Fields. This is because this section of the village is secluded and is accessed via a quiet lane. It's an ideal spot to commit a criminal act. Horribly, in six years' time, Uncle Dan's mother my Nan would live in sheltered accommodation close to these spots.

After our walk, I make a nutmeg cake and Dad loses his temper at the dinner table. Food ends up on the floor. As usual, noisy life events takes the spotlight.

ROUTE 6: **18 May 1980: Mount St. Helen's and Horrid Dreams**

Mum, Mazie, a friend and I walk towards Foxton Village.

24

Seven days after my walk over Tolshin Fields with Dad and Eve, Mum walks me down Fox Road with Mazie and a friend. After encountering one assault site, I am encountering another. We walk past the Barracks but am unsure of the remaining route (shown grey). We return to the cottage via a main road to the northwest of the village.

On the morning of our walk, Mount St. Helen's had erupted. Seeing news reports of smothering pyroclastic clouds had triggered subconscious notions of heat and suffocation in my toddlerhood. Indeed, on the 21st, I remark on this eruption. I grew obsessed with survival stories, particularly lone ones. I seldom remarked on current affairs in my diaries. As can be seen from my entries, I have a preoccupation with nature's fury including volcanoes.

Around this time, I am frantically tidying the playhouse. I install lino and have tea in there a few times, likely with Eve. I have taken up rugging now. Another diversion.

On 20th May, (two days after walking over these fields and the St Helen's eruption) I report of having 'horrid dreams'.

ROUTE 7: 21 July 1980: Transformation of My Diary

A lone walk part-way to Foxton.

On this day, I walked a little way down Fox Road. A day ago, (20 July) I have begun my highly-detailed diary. A wealth of information can now be found within. I believe this is the doing of my plural. She wants clues to my toddlerhood reported in my diaries, and a small one is insufficient.

The Moscow Olympics had begun two days ago. 1968 was an Olympic year too and has shown to bring triggers. The day after this walk, I ask about my ancestors. This appears to be a repeat of my behaviour on the 24th and 25th of July 1978 when I sneak into Dad's room after a bike ride: I look in the family bible. I'm looking into my past after venturing over an assault site. A day after this walk, I buy a barometer. This purchase reflects my preoccupation with nature's fury, air pressure and cyclones. This is because vertigo and air deprivation embody suffocation.

25 -31 Aug 1980: The Three Jaunts

At the end of August, I go on two jaunts to the east of the village. The first is described here.

ROUTE 8: 25 Aug 1980: Living the Lie

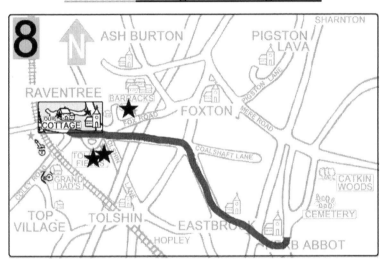

I cycle to Kerb Abbot with Dad and Eve.

I am frantically hobbying (I have taken up jogging, an astronomy project and now toy-making) but my hobbying steps-up after this first bike ride of August 1980. I have encountered Kerb Abbot of the big church with the burial ground of the past stowed out of sight. We would return via Dad's garage not far from Tolshin Fields.

That day, a wheelchair-bound girl called Donna Jenkins comes round and Dad gets a soaking from a hosepipe during a water fight. I am playing 'happy families' while my plural watches in the shadows after I had been to the Land of Berks. A year later, Donna would disclose she had been raped. I would then be triggered into writing a lengthy mystery thriller.

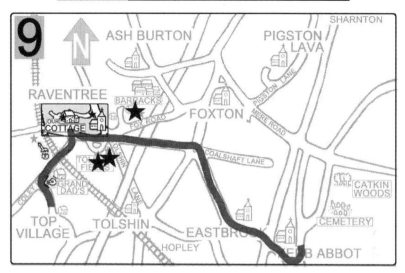

A walk with Mum down Coley Road to Top Village and a drive to Kerb Abbot.

The day after my trip to Kerb Abbot, Mum, Eve and I go blackberry picking on Coley Road. Finding little, we venture to Top Village which offered little more. In the end, we go via car to Kerb Abbot where we find loads and Mum makes a pie later that day.

Kerb Abbot's profusion of blackberries could be perceived as a payoff for backing berk-land, but the truth always seeps out. I had remarked in my diary on several hot air balloons drifting over our garden that day. 'I could hear the flames,' (I had written). In other words, forceful bursts of air. This is the sound of someone trying to breathe. The next day (27 Aug), I suffer inexplicable abdominal cramps. I'm unpicking my fur jacket to make snails and a toy poodle. I got this jacket (and guitar) from Aunt Maud's daughter on 8 March 1978. In other words, Uncle Dan's only full niece. Later that day, I'm playing dolls with comatose Sue.

ROUTE 10: **1 Sept 1980: Marathon Man**

After my first day back at school (I describe it as horrible) I go blackberry picking with Mum down Coley Road. Again, we find none. Later I watch the film, *Marathon Man* (1976) starring Laurence Olivier and Dustin Hoffman. A key scene shows a victim's mouth being forced open by a malevolent force. I had walked past a spot where Granddad had burnt his face and where I had found a skull. I then watch a film about head trauma.

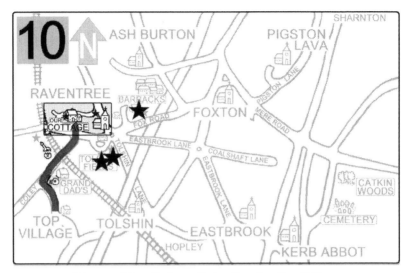

Mum and I walk down Coley Road to Top Village

That evening, Eve and I squabble about our bedroom light. I wanted it on. I always wanted the bedroom light on, and in the mid-Seventies, avoided my bed, sleeping in Mum's room instead. Over the following few days, I'm devising a lot of doll pantos with my sisters and making toys. I recall feeling terribly unsettled and grief-stricken. As can be seen, mementoes of head trauma in toddlerhood are fuelling my behaviour.

ROUTE 11: **22 Sept 1980: The Broken Mirror and the Missing Twin**

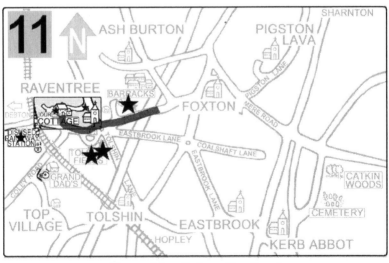

Eve and I walk down Fox Road.

Eve and I have a row and she broke my mirror. After she leaves the room, I pick it up to encounter my broken reflection. I threw the mirror away. The adage that a broken reflection will bring bad luck was for me superstitious nonsense and I took no notice. But like the skull near Granddad's and the *Marathon Man* film, my broken reflection had resounded with head trauma and becoming a plural.

Three decades later, I would write about a man perturbed by his reflection in a child's mirror. This novel, *The Locked Door* (2007-16) was a kidnap thriller I had written in my forties. I would fail to see how this scene relates to anything to do with me. My broken reflection in 1980 was behind the writing of this scene and I hadn't realised. I have since uncovered strands of innocence-lost in my Noughties novels as well as my Seventies children's mysteries.

Losing the Self

After Eve goes missing, I go in search for her in Debton, the next town. I traverse the disused railway station to get there. The day is dull and cold. I can't find her. I feel a deep dread. This is because I had confused my twin for my plural. I had encountered my broken face in the mirror and then my 'twin' goes missing. Little did I realise that my subconscious has been gleaning various ways of expressing the broken self from real life. My dread is of losing her.

News eventually comes that Eve has been caught shoplifting in Woolworths. She has been shoplifting a while by now. She is detained at the station while Mum retires to bed distraught. That afternoon, I take Eve for a walk down Fox Road towards the flyover. Why would I do this? The answer is I have just encountered my broken face in the mirror before my 'other self' goes missing. After venturing over the disused railway station in search for her, I would walk her down Fox Road. I believe my subconscious had drawn me to assault sites of my toddlerhood where I am joined to my plural. But having an identical twin has confused me.

Delayed Response

I spend the next day working on my meteorology project. I'm still making toys (a teddy bear now) and play dolls. My subconscious is continually aggravated by notions of my toddlerhood.

Eve exhibits her own response that evening. She came over nauseous (we were playing dolls) and everyone assumes it's shock from the arrest. I now suspect it is a delayed response to encountering a trauma site the previous afternoon (Fox Road). Big Sue of our doll pantos was roleplaying a comatose toddler too. In toddlerhood, Eve may have seen me being raped by Uncle Dan on the roadside. As we are identical twins and she had been orally raped too, would have physically empathised.

ROUTE?: 29 Dec 1980: Echoes of Burnt on Ash

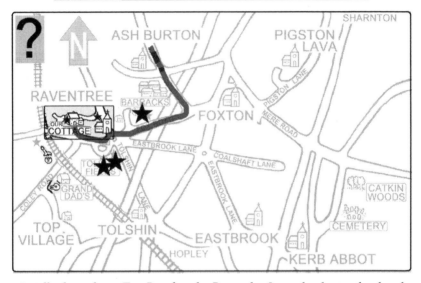

I walk alone down Fox Road to the Barracks. I turn back at a dead end.

My diary entry is rather sketchy here, but I have supplied a map of what I can find.

After suffering cabin fever over the Christmas period, I walked alone down Fox Road and turn off towards the Barracks. The dead end I describe in my diary is likely Ash Burton, as the road peters out in this quiet village. I notice the 'bur't-on ash' of Ash Burton(n). My plural has picked up on this placename (and others like it), for such proper nouns with a burnt slant are rife in my stories. This walk is a repeat behaviour of my walk on 30 Dec 1977 (and 22 Sept 1980), for being triggered.

The Barracks and the Keep Out Signs

The Barracks are located on a quiet lane off Fox Road. I hadn't been there much, but the place would leave an impression. The Barracks are surrounded with high wire fences with 'keep out' signs everywhere. My subconscious has twisted these words to become that of a 'doorkeeper'. By this, I mean the part of my mind that hides the truth from me. I am banished from the traumas of my toddlerhood. 'Keep out'.

Echoes of 1968

I return from this walk so cold, my legs itched. I make dinner that evening because Mum isn't feeling well herself. That night, I couldn't sleep and skip breakfast. I'm up early and have trouble revising for my mock O Levels (I'm revising in Dad's room). Nan is stopping over Christmas and gets a little drunk so Mum and I help her to bed. My oldest sister's children are stopping too. They are blond, aged 3 and 5 respectively. The situation bears startling parallels to Christmas 1968.

Nan had stopped over Christmas then too, and like my sister's children, Eve and I were blonde toddlers. It is leap year. The missing piece is Uncle Dan, for he was stopping at the cottage too, but instead of sleeping in the guestroom that became Dad's (as he did for most of 1968), he was sleeping in a small bedroom next to ours. In 1980, it was Nicholas's. Due to the children stopping, I have to sleep in that very room. I have slept in there before and felt horribly disturbed.

These notions of an earlier time seem to explain my walk down Fox Road.

JAUNTS OF 1981

7 June 1981: Jungle Mural, Lemurs and the Elms

The opening bike ride of 1981 is little described, hence no map, but I report of a ten-mile bike ride with Dad and Eve beginning with Fox Road. This bike ride involves a piece of artwork, one of my many creative pursuits. Like my toy pantos and children's mysteries, my artwork hides clues to my toddlerhood.

On 6th June, I prepare hardboard in my bedroom for a painting which I would call *Jungle Mural*. It would be my biggest painting yet, at 4x2ft. On the same day, Mum gets me a book on hurricanes and twisters. I would spend all evening reading it. The next day (7th June) is Whitsun Pentecost and I'm teaching at Sunday School. The theme is Adam and Eve and the Creation. Afterwards, I would go on this bike ride.

A week later, my 4x2ft panel would become *Jungle Mural* (17-25 June). For years to come, I would paint jungle scenes. They are not what they appear.

This is how *Jungle Mural* relates to my bike rides.

31

Road signs seen on my bike rides and walks. The 'me' slashed in two: elm, elm-hurts, I-elm. and the keep out signs that form the division. The bottom image shows the two lemurs in my Jungle Mural *painting. These mean 'you are elms'.*

The Elm of a slashed Me

Jungle Mural shows two lemurs in a tree. The word 'lemur' is an anagram of u-r-elm. You are elm. An elm is 'me' (spelled backwards) with a slash between.

Me. Em. Elm.

A slashed me.

This elm-thing is echoed throughout my creations.

The word 'elm' has been seen on bike routes in various ways. An Elmhurst Farm exists outside Kerb Abbot; The Elms can be found near Tolshin Fields and Ash Burton. Mile Tree means I-elm teer (or tear). The elm appears in my novels too: Elmhurst is in *The Lessons* and means 'elm-hurts'. It's hurts to be a plural. The Elms also appear in my final novel, *Nadia*. The 'keep out' signs mark the division between us.

It's like the broken mirror of 22nd Sept 1980 – another way of expressing a slashed 'me', and my plural is garnering from life, these expressions without my conscious awareness. Seeing these things is like holding a mirror to the self.

Conclusion of Jaunts Instigated by Others (30 April 1977 – 7 June 1981)

Thus far, my jaunts to the east of the village have (largely) been instigated by others. For the first time since toddlerhood, I am encountering assault sites on foot or bike. Responses would follow. I suffer emotional upsets and depression, unsettled nights, horrid dreams, inexplicable illnesses, sudden bursts of creative outpouring and a desire to delve into the past. Finally, I would encounter landmarks and placenames that (for my plural) has hidden meanings.

The time covered so far is 30 April 1977 – 7 June 1981. From 8 July 1981 onwards, I would instigate my jaunts with Eve. The trigger would become the triggered behaviour. The question now is, what triggers the jaunt itself?

Jungle Mural. *Clues to my toddlerhood are rife in this painting, such as the lion mounting the stag, the lemurs and the butterfly. The surroundings echoes of Privy Woods. The leopard means leper'd as in outcast due to the 'snake'.*

33

3. Jaunts Instigated by Me
(8 July 1981 – 17 Oct 1986)

In July 1981, Eve and I have just turned sixteen and have left school. We feel capable of going on jaunts by ourselves. The dynamics are different now. What was once a trigger has now become the response. This is because these trips are driven by me, no one else. These self-instigated jaunts begin with profusion – ten bike rides in July 1981. How odd. I wouldn't instigate another until 22nd Nov of that year.

ROUTE 12: **8 July 1981: Butterfly Mural and 3 Bike Rides in a Day**

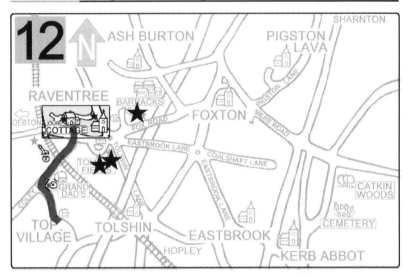

Eve and I cycle down Coley Road to Top Village.

Today, Eve and I go on three bike rides. The first is to Debton via the disused railway station (to get oil paints), the second is unreported, and the third is to Top Village via Coley Road (where Granddad used to live). The third jaunt is shown on the map.

Between 3-13 July, I would complete another mural. This one is the same size as *Jungle Mural* and is called *Butterfly Mural* which again, hides clues to my toddlerhood. Fly agarics proliferate while bloody-coloured butterflies take off. During the painting of *Butterfly Mural*, Eve and I went on these bike rides. Dad no longer accompanies us.

After these bike rides, I feverishly painted *Butterfly Mural* in the corner of the bedroom. I did the 'red butterfly and the fly agaric,' (I had written in my diary). It seems I am briefly sharing Eve's preoccupation with fungi

34

for something I had seen in toddlerhood. On the 10th of July, I suffer a terrible period pain and go to bed.

15-21 July 1981: Six Bike Rides

Over seven days, Eve and I go on six further bike rides. Most are to the east of the village and all are instigated by me. I have just completed *Butterfly Mural* (3-13 July) and had suffered a terrible period pain (10 July). I then go overboard with these bike rides, as described here.

ROUTE 13: 15 July 1981: Shambury and the Barracks

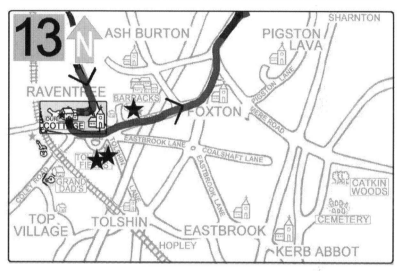

Eve and I cycle through Foxton towards Sharnton. We get lost and return via a main road on the northwest.

Eve and I got lost on our bike ride. 'We took a wrong turning for the motorway, (I had written). Ended up seeing signs for Shanbury and the Barracks. We were lost. Went down a main road. We must've gone twenty-five miles. Enjoyed it in a way.'

This appears to be sabotage, as Dad had given clear directions that morning and we had been on these routes before. The ride was supposed to end as we had begun: Fox Road. Instead, we get lost and are gone almost three hours. Mum went mad when we got back.

Sham Bury and Keep Out

I report in my diary that I had seen signs for Shanbury and the Barracks. *Shanbury?* No Shanbury exists in the area, but a village called Sharnton does. Evidently, I had got the name mixed up on writing it in my diary putting 'Shanbury' instead of Sharnton. But Shanbury sounds like 'sham bury'. I am a sham bury(ing) the past. Indeed, the 'bury' suffix recurs in placenames of my stories. Furthermore, the Barracks was remarked upon for associations with the 'keep out' signs. To my plural, these road signs echo the message of an inner doorkeeper: Bury the past and keep out. The result is that I had got lost and would fail to return via an assault site. After this bike ride, I showed my murals to Mazie's friends.

ROUTE 14: **16 July 1981: Bike Maintenance**

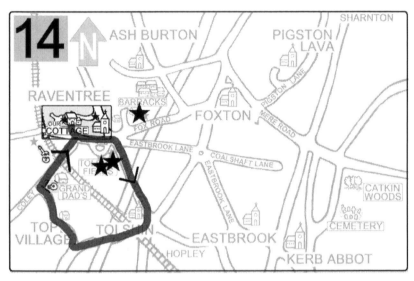

Eve and I cycle to Tolshin and Top Village, returning via Coley Road

The day after getting lost on my bike ride, I had 'an awful dream. Worst of this year,' (I had written). This is because of what happened the day before. An assault site had agitated my subconscious, then an inner doorkeeper had shouted at me via road signs.

Still, I would take Eve on another bike ride that morning on a more usual route. Afterwards, we spruced up our bikes. I took the front wheel off, sandpapered the rust and tarted it up with metallic paint. My bike had been orange with yellow tape. It is now lilac with blue tape. I was pleased with the new look. This is because I had overlaid the hot colours with cool ones. I'm burying the past again. Meanwhile, Dad takes Eve's chain off. (Interestingly, Eve's bike is all-over red). We leave our bikes under the playhouse porch to dry. I then write to Nan.

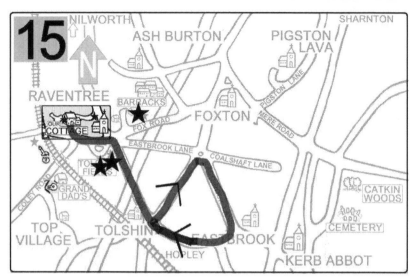

Eve and I cycle down Tolshin Lane, Eastbrook, Hopley and Tolshin, returning via Tolshin Lane.

Two days after tarting up our bikes, Eve and would I go on another long bike ride. Afterwards, we did some shopping with the family in Nilworth, a large town northwest of the village. Eve cries. I don't say why. That evening, Eve and I squabble because I wanted the bedroom door ajar, so the landing light can shine through. It seems these bike rides are stirring horrible dreams and I'm scared of the dark. Today I had begun and ended my bike ride with the Tolshin Lane assault site.

I end my diary entry with my typical weather description. 'Clear morning, mediocris developing stratocumulus. Bright sunny spells, warm with cool breezy spells. Dry. At dark there was lovely moon rising from the east. Gold then silver as it rose. Large.'

ROUTE?: **19 July 1981: Two Bike Rides in a Day**

On the 19th July, I remark in my diary that I wanted to take Eve on the 'twenty-five-mile bike ride' (the one of 15th July where I had got lost and saw signs for Sham-bury and the Barracks) but 'didn't have the heart.' Instead, we go on two short ones, each an hour long. The first was to Top Village and Tolshin (shown dark); the second was down Eastbrook Lane (show grey). Details are sketchy in my diary as directions contradict one other, hence the question mark.

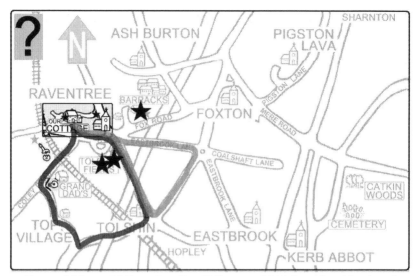

Eve and I have 2 bike rides: Top Village and Tolshin; then Eastbrook Lane, returning via Tolshin Lane.

Still, I'm not going the doorkeeper way. I had ridden past an assault site (Tolshin Lane) likely twice. I would continue to encounter placenames and landmarks that trigger notions of my toddlerhood for assault sites, being a sham, a plural and sensations of trauma.

ROUTE 16: 21 July 1981: Possible Bike Sabotage

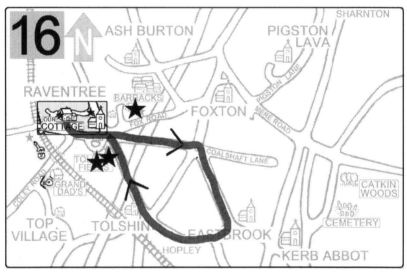

Eve and I cycle to Eastbrook and Tolshin, returning via Tolshin Lane

Eve and I go swimming that morning before going on our sixth bike ride in a week. Eve's bike chain came off twice during the trip. On the 16th of July, I report of taking my front wheel off to tart up the spokes while Dad takes Eve's chain off.

This seems to link to the jaunt of 3rd April 1982 when Eve's pedal mysteriously comes off (this incident is explained under the date concerned). But sabotage of our bike rides would come under question. Evidently, a part of me is averse to these bike rides and might be picking up ideas on how to stop them. Things going missing or wrong would recur in other areas of my life for the same reason: to keep me away from my toddlerhood. If so, this system is automated and completely without my conscious awareness. Here, I had ended the ride via the Tolshin Lane assault site.

ROUTE 17: **30 July 1981: Local Child Killer**

Eve and I cycle to Foxton and Eastbrook, returning via Eastbrook Lane.

In the height of summer, Dad is tarting up the cottage. He is wallpapering and replacing glass in the garret and doors. I'm painting the radiators and Eve is painting the sliding door. On 28th of July, I report in my diary, 'There's a child killer on the loose in the next town. They found a green car belonging to him.' The next day, I report of sleeplessness. I watched Charles and Di's wedding on TV then spend a sunny afternoon on a small swing in the back garden with Nicholas.

On the 30th July, after getting wallpaper, I take Eve on this bike ride, which I report to be 'nice'. For the second time this month, I had wheeled past the Fox Road assault site. We return to see Dad painting the ceilings. His temper is bubbling beneath the surface, but I help Mum prepare her jumble sale, used to the atmosphere. In future years, reports relating to child atrocities and rape has shown to trigger me into visiting my past.

This would be my final bike ride that summer.

ROUTE 18: **22 Nov 1981: Male Attention at a Student Party**

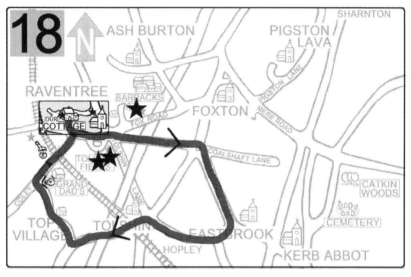

Eve and I cycle to Eastbrook, Tolshin and Top Village, returning via Coley Road.

Four months have gone by before I instigate another jaunt – a bike ride with Eve on 22nd Nov. 'Nearly killed myself, (I had written in my diary). I was puffed out and my legs were like jelly afterwards.' I'm obviously out of shape. Oddly this bike ride goes nowhere near an assault site, but cuts through the 'mock' one of Coley Road. I am devising Christmas calendars depicting local scenes, including the Weavers pub near Fox Road and the back of the church near Privy Woods. I am now in my first term of art college, having left school. I am still sixteen.

The timing of this ride seems odd. It is late November and I hadn't been on one since 30th July. Why would I go now? The evening previous (21 Nov), I had received significant male attention at a student party (two boys chat me up). I had never received such attention before. Prior to this party, Mum had left a note to get hair dye for her. I plan to get a birthday present at the same time. Things go missing, hampering my chances of going to the party. Something is trying to stop me from going (just like the bike rides) because of possible triggers. I manage to go in the end. The house is throbbing and smoke-filled. I return to college the following Monday where this boy finally asks me out. I feel irritable that evening and go for a walk with Eve in the village to settle myself. By horrible coincidence, I start my period on the same day as my first date with my boyfriend (24 Nov). I feel nauseous. This, my second ever boyfriend, is stocky-built with thick, dark hair, like Uncle Dan, but lacked his height. My plural was obviously unsettled by comparisons.

My first boyfriend had finished with me just a few weeks ago. He was dark too, only taller. I can't seem to sustain a boyfriend. I am told something about me is 'different'.

It appears my bike ride was triggered by male attention at a party.

JAUNTS OF 1982

It is now 1982.My diary is my biggest yet, a tome A4 in size. Like the previous spring, bike rides and walks are copious. Between 20 March and 16 April 1982, I report of ten jaunts to the east of the village.

On 5th April, something extraordinary happens. The following describes the lead up.

12 Feb 1982: The Postponement

I'm painting *Face of the Tiger* (31 Jan-12 Feb 1982) in my bedroom – another jungle painting it seems. Interestingly, on the day I begin this painting, Eve goes on a bike ride alone, which is unusual for her. I don't know where she goes. Meanwhile, I am suffering all sorts of bewildering and horrible symptoms such as headaches, upset stomachs and depression. I skive from college a few times. This is because my outpourings have grown profuse: Clues to my horrific toddlerhood are pouring into my college artwork, I'm about to embark upon a momentous project about natural disasters and my plural has a huge diary to express herself – a far cry from those of 1979 and 1980.

Strangely, *Face of the Tiger* has no bearing upon my art course at all. For years, I have been painting and drawing for my own reasons and this was no different.

I complete *Face of the Tiger* on the 12th of Feb.

41

On the day I finish this painting, I tell Eve I plan to take my youngest sister Mazie secretly on a bike ride with us. Mazie is at this time, eight and Mum would have gone mad if she knew. For now, my plan was postponed, but I kept this bike ride in mind for the future. I was determined to take her.

20 March 1982: Chronic Illnesses Descend

My secret bike ride remains on my mind, but for now, I decide to take Eve alone. I don't say where but am certain it is my usual eastern jaunt beginning with Fox Road. Earlier that day, I had suffered an incredible depression. I feel trapped and the cottage is shabby. The old Anglia is a wreck and there's nothing to do. My niece and nephew are due to stop the night again and I often end up minding them. Before they come, I threw stuff about in a crying fit. Perhaps to clear the air, I ask Eve to go on a bike ride. Two days later (22 March), I become suddenly ill with a throat bug, stubborn phlegm, stiff neck, headache and dizziness. Clues to my toddlerhood have never come so thick and fast and I would fail to see a thing.

ROUTE 19: 28 March 1982: Leopard Lily and Other Leopards

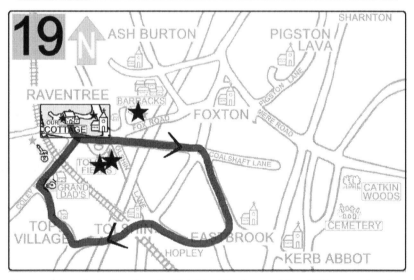

Eve and I cycle to Eastbrook, Tolshin, Hopley and Top Village, returning via Coley Road.

It is late March and my throat is still playing up. I report, 'It is terribly tickly, I can't sleep, I have a blocked nose and discomfort in stomach. I'm breathless'. I'm doing a lot of stuff about tornadoes and hurricanes in a weather project I've been working on since 28th Feb (superseding earlier ones) and I'm still producing a lot of artwork. The old Ford Anglia is finally scrapped. On 27th March, I begin drawing a leopard lily cactus for my art diploma. I have just completed another jungle scene, this one showing a leopard and lion against a stratocumulus sky. I am now about to draw Mum's dining room clock. These 'leper'd' artworks with artefacts of a forgotten cottage are informing upon my horrific toddlerhood in surreptitious ways. As if this workload isn't enough, I'm producing church posters for Palm Sunday and the Crucifixion. Mum often involves me in church matters.

On impulse I prepare our bikes and ask Eve to come out. This ride leaves me depressed, as I report, 'the sun gave a sad light, misty sky. It glowed through the foggy veil like a cool globe.' It put me off bike rides for a while. This jaunt echoes that of 22nd Nov 1981, for going nowhere near an assault site. But Coley Road remains a potent mock one, for the skull, broken artifacts, an exile's hut and Granddad's burnt face.

3 – 16 April 1982: Seven Bike Rides and a Walk

After a slow start, my bike rides gather. Again, my subconscious is suddenly drawn to my toddlerhood assault sites, but another part of me doesn't want me to go. My secret bike ride for Mazie is anon and what happens that day is bewildering.

ROUTE 20: 3 April 1982: The Beginning of Easter

It is the first day of the Easter holidays and Eve and I go on a bike ride. I have a shower beforehand and my abdomen cramps up. I'm nowhere near a period. I have suffered these inexplicable cramps for years and would suffer them for years to come. I assume my old mattress needs changing or I'm not sleeping right.

Meanwhile Eve and I cycle past the Tolshin Lane assault site and the mock one of Coley Road. I report of the wind against us and Eve fell over. We end our ride by sitting in a driveway.

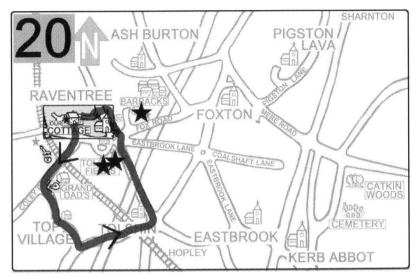

Eve and I cycle down Coley Road, Top Village, Tolshin and Tolshin Lane

Eve, Mazie and I then plan our secret bike ride. I decided upon Eastbrook Lane with a picnic, but as will be seen, I would change my mind twice. That evening, Eve and Mazie went to a club with Dad. I stop at home and watch TV.

ROUTE 21: 4 April 1982: Eve's Pedal Comes Off

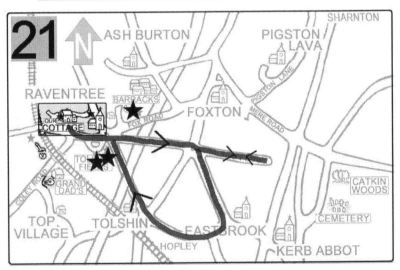

Eve and I cycle down Eastbrook Lane to Coalshaft Lane. We retrace and ride through Eastbrook, Hopley and Tolshin, returning via Tolshin Lane.

The day after Eve had gone out with Dad, Nan (my uncle's mother) comes to stay and I'm writing notes on the weather. I'm suffering a stiff neck in the morning. I ask Dad for ideas for a new bike ride. He suggests Kerb Abbot and Foxton, but again, I would dither.

Instead, I report of riding down Eastbrook Lane to Coalshaft Lane. Coalshaft Lane ends on a farmer's gate. I report that Eve and I sat on a fence at this dead end. 'It was lovely, (I had written). It was really deserted, our secret place.' We remained for twenty minutes before retracing our way and riding through Eastbrook. *Our secret place?* What did I mean by that?

At Hopley, Eve's pedal feels 'tender'. She wants to turn back. But here, I would select a picnic spot where I would take Mazie. We return via Tolshin Lane where Eve's pedal finally comes off. She has to scoot the rest of the way.

Once home, Dad had a look at Eve's bike crank. Nicholas and I teased her about it. In the evening, I'm writing about earthquakes on my bed while Eve goes out with a school friend.

Bike Rides Interrupted

The matter of Eve's pedal troubles me. I've seen Dad fiddle with our bikes and I can do basic maintenance. Could I have sabotaged her bike to prevent us from going on our secret picnic? Did our bike ride of 21st July 1981 (when her chain came off) provide the idea? I don't like to think so, but the opportunity for sabotage had arisen the night before: when Eve, Dad and Mazie had gone to a club. If this is so, I have no recollection of touching her bike or of sabotaging anything.

Of further note is the secret place of Coalshaft Lane. I have since been up there, and the ambience at the dead end is strongly evocative of Fox Road. The gate faces the same way and the landscape has an echoing quality. I had called it our 'secret place'. I'm not talking about Eve, but my plural. It resembles an assault site where I am joined to my plural.

ROUTE 22: **5 April 1982: The Secret Bike Ride with Picnic**

Today would be my secret bike ride I had planned on 12th Feb (the day I had completed *Face of the Tiger)*. I'm up at 5.50am to 'a lovely cloudy morning filled with bird sound,' (I had written). I packed a picnic and waited until 1.30pm when Mum was out of the way. Eve, Mazie and I venture out. Sabotage or not, my planned jaunt has finally become reality.

45

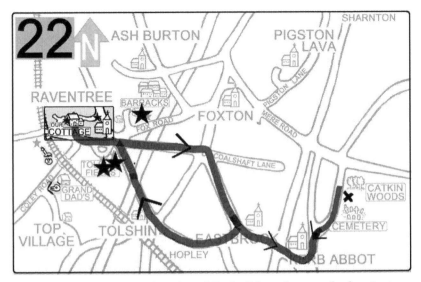

Eve and I cycle to Eastbrook and Kerb Abbot where we had a picnic (marked with the 'X'). We continue to Hopley and Tolshin. We return via Tolshin Lane.

Oddly, I didn't take Mazie to Eastbrook Lane or Hopley, but Kerb Abbot (Dad's suggestion yesterday). At times, Mazie lags behind. She is just eight. Our picnic spot would occur outside the Land of Berks. I had written in my diary, 'We lifted our bikes over a fence (meaning gate) and sat on the grass. A bee came and we rushed out, so we sat on the opposite side of the road by a tree (where another gate is situated). I jumped over a ditch. We sat on the grass on our coats and ate.'

Our spot is between the cemetery and Catkin Woods.

We complete our jaunt by returning to Eastbrook, cutting through Hopley (my previous decision for a picnic) and Tolshin Lane. When I got home, I wrote about earthquakes (like I had last night). The next day, a headache descends. Not feeling 'too high,' (I had written). Mum perms my hair that evening. The day after that (7th April), I'm writing about volcanoes.

I am bewildered at what I have done. Evidently, I had projected my younger self upon Mazie, and my plural upon my twin.

The following images clarify.

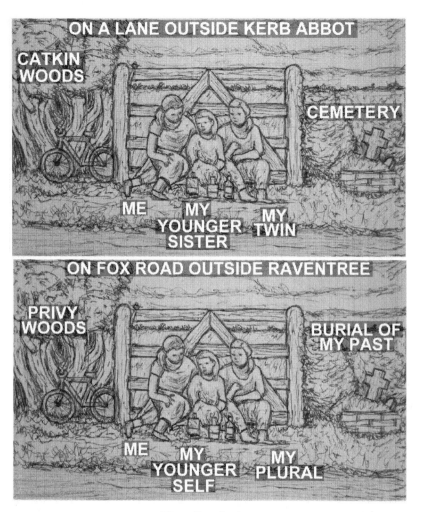

ON A LANE OUTSIDE KERB ABBOT

CATKIN WOODS

CEMETERY

ME MY YOUNGER SISTER MY TWIN

ON FOX ROAD OUTSIDE RAVENTREE

PRIVY WOODS

BURIAL OF MY PAST

ME MY YOUNGER SELF MY PLURAL

The Confusion

The images show a reconstruction of our secret picnic. The cemetery and Catkins Woods outside Kerb Abbot are shown close together for illustration purposes, but are in fact a mile apart.

The upper image shows a routine picnic with my twin and youngest sister in a quiet spot just outside Kerb Abbot.

The lower image gives a different story. I am joining with my plural via my eight-year-old self (of 1972 when I had encountered a replica of Privy Woods). We are outside the 'Land of Berks' on the reverse side of the burial ground where my past has been unearthed. Privy Woods is just up the road and we are sitting at the foot of the Fox Road gate. I am going

47

back in time, joining with my plural towards 1968 via my younger self. Only through my younger self can my toddlerhood be reached.

This is how my plural sees this event and she is trying to tell me about my toddlerhood. Sadly, recall would fail, as it had done so in Catkin Woods in 1972. I had felt unsettled by those woods but didn't know why.

Echoes of Assault Sites

The images stitch together the events of 3-5 April 1982 (photos taken September 2020). Shown are farmers' gates I had considered for my picnic spot.

Top row: Two gates on Eastbrook Lane (my initial choices).

Middle row (from left): My 'secret place' of Coalshaft Lane and a gate at Hopley (where Eve's pedal had come off).

Bottom row: Two gates outside Kerb Abbot. We would picnic on the one shown left before a bee had driven us off and we resituate on a gate on the opposite side of the road (shown right). The nature of PTSD means I am continually reminded of the past and such gates, open hedges and farmers' fields would draw my attention.

The assault site is a farmer's gate on Fox Road (picture taken Sept 2020).

This site echoes countless gates and open hedges in the countryside that stirs something within me. This gate on Fox Road is just a few minutes' walk from the cottage and is where I was raped at the age of three.

Wherever I see gates in open hedges and fields like this, I sense something is waiting for me and I want to go there. My jaunts of 1985 would dispel any doubts I had been raped on this spot at the age of three.

8 April 1982: My Illnesses Close In

I have briefly joined with my plural at a ghost assault site.

Health niggles swoop in with bad throat, crampy stomach and headache.

Today, I feel terrible. I rouse with a heavy head, dizzy spells and achy joints. I had first reported of a stiff neck on the 4th of April when Eve's pedal had come off. Despite how I felt, I talked Eve into going for a bike ride to Foxton and the Barracks (with the 'keep out' signs). We reached the Weavers pub when Eve complained it was cold. When I got back, I ran upstairs feeling terrible and collapsed on my bed. I'm reading *Element's Rage* and stuff about volcanoes and tornadoes again. I retire to bed early with a temperature and get little sleep until late.

On 9th April, I'm feeling worse. I had planned to attend the 2.15pm Good Friday Service at church, but I felt so sick. I got a jigsaw down instead – a 200-piece showing Big Ben. I reported in my diary, 'I curled up on the chair and my sickness climaxed. Had no dinner. Nan said my throat showed signs of bleeding. My neck is stiff and everything aches. I feel dizzy with loud banging in my ears.' I tried Andrews to settle my stomach but it didn't work.

The next day, I'm still feeling bad. On 11th April (Easter Sunday) A cough roused me early. I manage to go to church with Mum, Nan and my siblings. Later, a programme about a trapped, dying whale in Newfoundland made me cry.

A part of me doesn't want me going on these bike rides and another wants disclosure. Despite everything, the truth keeps rearing up and I'm prevented from seeing it. Never did I think these illness could be a response to getting close to my toddlerhood at all. But in future years, such illnesses would strike when faced with further mementoes like these.

ROUTE 23: 13 April 1982: Crack in the World

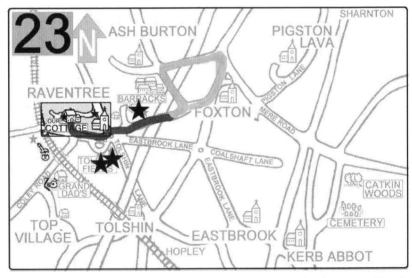

Eve and I walk down Fox Road, aiming for the Barracks, but turned back.

My secret picnic of 5th April continues to reverberate and I'm still feeling ill. On the 12th April, I watched a film with Nan called *Crack in the World* (1965). This would be the third time I would see it, being one of my favourites. This film enthralled me, but others didn't seem to share my view. I was forever watching disaster movies. Afterwards, I got irritable. Dad took Eve and me to the pictures to watch *Chariots of Fire* (prequelled by *Gregory's Girl*). My throat is still tickly. On the 13th, I report my sleep is 'full of dreams'. That morning, I urged Eve to go for a walk to the Barracks with me but she didn't feel up to it. We go no further than the flyover on Fox Road before we turned back. A doorkeeper in my head is trying to remind me of the 'keep out' signs but I never got to see them. Watching a film about a severed world (mine) isn't helping matters.

By a horrid coincidence, Dad called us to his bedroom to show us some slides after our walk.

ROUTE 24: **14 April 1982: Nuclear War and the Weather Book**

Eve and I cycle to Eastbrook Lane to Coalshaft Lane and back.

On the following day (14th April), I awoke in the middle of the night (3am) after a horrible dream about nuclear war. I was in fact dreaming of assault. I am seeing the sunburst on the eastbound lane close-up, the crack in the earth and the fuel behind my earthquake and volcano stuff.

This is the consequence of coming too close to my inner toddler, and such responses continue decades on. No wonder I have a plural!

That day, I got the *Observer's Book of Weather* by Robert Pierce and began reading it. I have an earlier *Observer's book on Weather*, this one by Reginal M Lester. I loved that book. The image on the cover had drawn me. It was of a cumulonimbus mushrooming over the ocean. It resembles a nuclear explosion – a bit like my horrible dream. After getting this book, I took Eve on our bike ride to Coalshaft Lane (my 'secret place'). I report of reaching a farmhouse where the road got rough. I note another placename that reverberates for my plural: 'coal' (as in burn) and shaft (as in buried). The cottage of the Seventies had coal fires and I must have stared at the embers with subconscious notions of burning. Once we got home, I continue reading my weather book and cried in bed.

ROUTE 25: 15 April 1982: The Best Bike Ride

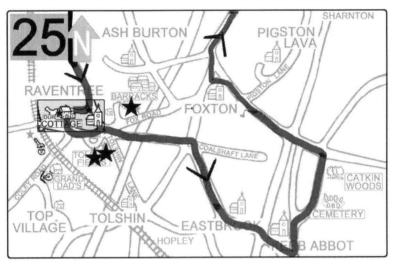

Eve and I cycle to Eastbrook and Kerb Abbot, pausing at Catkin Woods. We cut through Foxton and return via the northwest of the village.

Today is hot and I've started my periods. I report it was 'light and symptom-free' which was unusual for me. With persistent illnesses and feeling sick, I must have lost weight, curtailing blood flow and cramps. Still, I report this was one of my best bike rides yet. I wanted to take my radio but Eve told me not to bother.

For the first time since 5th April, I would take Eve to Kerb Abbot. We would wheel past the little cemetery and my secret picnic spot. We would then stop at Catkin Woods. Today, we would do the same thing as we had one September day in 1972: pick pussy willow and catkins. We must have encountered the clearing that had unsettled me ten years ago. We would conclude our trip by returning to the cottage from the northwest. We don't encounter an actual assault site at all but an echo of Privy Woods. I describe the bike ride as 'lovely'.

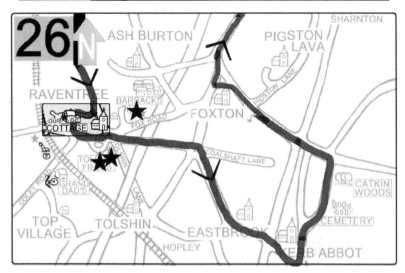

Eve and I cycle to Eastbrook, Kerb Abbot, Foxton and got lost on a main road. We return via the northwest of the village.

The following day, I seek out a repeat of our 'lovely' Kerb Abbot bike ride. I'm still reading my new weather book and have now discovered a monthly magazine called *Weather*. I wanted to order it but never did. We then go on our final bike ride of 1982. It wasn't so good. We encountered runners on Eastbrook Lane and a cyclist kept pestering us. We again cut through Kerb Abbot and stop at Catkin Woods and venture in. The weather is now cloudy and I feel threatened for some reason. This is because the weather was cloudy when I was assaulted in Privy Woods fourteen years ago. Recall comes close, but doesn't occur.

I had planned to end our ride via Fox Road but I got lost again (like on 15th July 1981). We found our way after I asked a woman for directions and noticed a sign for the Barracks (the place with the 'keep out' signs). But on a junction near home, a driver reprimanded me for not looking where I was going. This greatly upset me and I report in my diary, 'I can't cope with people.' Depression hits hard. The 'keep out' and the reprimand had been the reasons.

Keep Out and the Curtailment of Bike Rides

I can now see the words of this driver reflected an inner doorkeeper again. The woman had told me to 'watch where you are going!' In other words, keep away from your toddlerhood. No wonder. Reminders of the past are making me feel ill and depressed.

The following day, there is a terrible scene between Dad and Eve. Other siblings get involved trying to part them and we end up on the floor. I describe the scene as 'fucking awful.' Dad's outburst had been building up for ages because Mum appears to have turned her back on us. There is little food in and the place is shabby. She is forever involved with the church or other matters. On the 19th April, Mum starts work as a receptionist and would remain so until she retires eighteen years later. The day previous, Nan returns to Aunt Maud's. This would be my final bike ride of the year. Encounters with the past and an inner doorkeeper seems to have deterred me.

Still, something unexpected is about to happen: I would make my first report of telling Eve a 'silly story' about a 'John' on 23 April. By June, I was doodling his face. These disturbing stories and drawings are fuelled by my toddlerhood. On 23 April 1985, I would begin a novel, based on these stories. This novel would be called *The Lessons* and it would tell me about the disused railway station. The day I began this novel, I became ill.

An Interim in the Bike Rides and when I Begin Driving Lessons

I wouldn't go on another self-instigated jaunt for fourteen months. But on 25th June 1982, I have my first driving lesson. Two months had passed since this final bike ride of 1982. I am now seventeen. My initial driving instructor often took me to the east of the village.

The end of this book takes a brief look at my driving lessons.

In July, Eve and I stopped at Aunt Maud's for a month. On the 17th, I would meet Uncle Dan for the first time since my toddlerhood. Maud drove Eve, Nan and me to his house one afternoon and I didn't twig a thing. I saw a greying, yet imposing man and I described him as 'nice' in my diary. A day later, inexplicable depression descends. A part of me knew I had just met my rapist, yet my oblivion has the last say.

Conclusion of Jaunts Instigated by Me (8 July 1981 – 16 April 1982)

From 8th July 1981, my jaunts to the east of the village had become self-instigated. But all would peter out from 16 April 1982. This is what I have found so far.

My creative projects appear to time-in with my jaunts. On the day I complete *Face of the Tiger* (12 Feb 1982), I decide to go on my secret bike ride. I would go on further rides on completing other projects, such *as Leopard Lily* and *Tropical Jungle.* Throughout this period, I'm writing about nature's fury.

My health niggles close in with incidence. I suffer chronic head-colds, sore throats and sporadic abdominal cramps. My illnesses spike after our secret picnic when I join with my plural.

My troubled nights and depression continue. I want the landing light on, have horrible dreams and feel threatened for no apparent reason.

A force in my head seems to be warning me against these bike rides, with things going wrong, illnesses and suspected sabotage. I am finally put off bike rides on 16th April 1982 after a woman tells me off.

My plural reads meanings into placenames and landmarks, like the elms of a broken self and the 'keep out signs' of the Barracks. Such proper nouns would leach into my stories and artwork for decades.

Being self-instigated, my bike rides have become triggered behaviour, just like my creative projects. I take Eve on a bike ride shortly after I hear about a local child killer. Four months after no bike rides at all, I go on a one-off after receiving male attention at a student party.

From 16th April 1983, my jaunts to the east of the village have all but ended. But I would undergo another flurry of self-instigated bike rides in July 1985. The following looks at the few jaunts between these dates.

ROUTE 27: **10 October 1982: A Sponsored Walk**

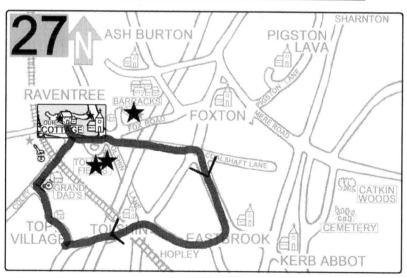

Eve and I did a 10-mile sponsored walk to Eastbrook, Hopley, Tolshin and Top Village. We return via Coley Road.

55

This jaunt was instigated by others – the church and is a ten-mile sponsored walk to raise money for the heating. I'm writing copious notes on tornadoes within a momentous weather project I had begun on 28th Feb 1982. We stop in a pub in Tolshin and I'm wary of male attention. Claps and whistling unsettle me. I'm now in my second year of my art diploma and am working on a zoo project. My big cat art is profuse.

JAUNTS OF 1983

The following year reports of only one bike ride with Eve (and a couple of walks) as shown here.

15 May 1983: I report of going on a long walk with Eve. I'm still writing copious notes on hurricanes and tornadoes, and have just included a section on Krakatoa. On the 10th of May, I had made my first encounter with Mark, an art student a year below me.

Mark was tall, broad and dark like Uncle Dan. I now realise, my plural has made comparisons with my childhood rapist, just like she had my other boyfriends. How awful. I then include a section on volcanoes in my weather project. This is due to notions of a man that burned me in toddlerhood.

But did this encounter with Mark spur a walk to an assault site? I'll never know, for my diary doesn't say.

30 May 1983: Mum instigates a walk down Coley Road towards Top Village. I mention the Barracks, but I don't think we walked there. (Mum and I had gone for a walk the day before to the northwest of the village). I'm drawing diagrams of tsunamis within my Krakatoa project and I'm taking photos of billowing cumulus clouds. That evening, I watch a late-night film called *When Time Ran Out* (1980) about a volcano.

Route 28: **19 June 1983: Vertigo, Blackout and Coma**

This bike ride is a one-off. I haven't instigated a bike ride to the east of the village since 16th April 1982 when a woman had told me to 'watch where you are going'. This jaunt is somewhat tame: going part-down Eastbrook Lane before I turn back. I go nowhere near an assault site or even a mock one. Still, what triggered this one-off?

That morning, Dad had suffered a nasty fall in the bathroom, blacking out and sustaining concussion. He bled from his scalp and the scab took ages to heal.

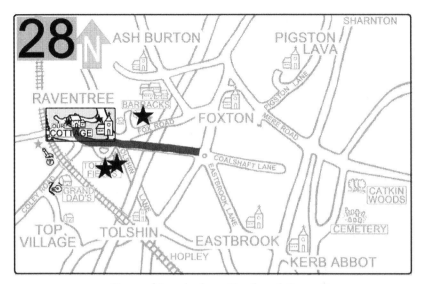

Eve and I cycle down Eastbrook Lane.

Eve and I are within an episode of portrait-doodling creepy characters in our sketchbooks (a compulsion which had been gathering since the 5th of June). On the 18th, I had stuck these portraits under Eve's pillow for a joke. The drawing would end up on next door's lawn after I had stuck it on the window. I'm taking sky photos with my new Praktica SLR camera, but my huge weather project is about to flounder. On the 10th of June, I had suffered terrible vertigo whilst writing about hurricane eyes.

I note Dad blacking out (into coma) that morning and my recent vertigo whilst writing about hurricane eyes. I'm drawing portraits of creepy men which are expressions of Uncle Dan. After this short bike ride, I wouldn't go on another in the area until 5th July 1985.

JAUNTS OF 1984

The year 1984 reports of only one jaunt to the east of the village, which is via car to a pub in Eastbrook.

26 Aug 1984: I went for a meal with Eve, Nicolas and a friend. I try to talk Nan out of going back to Aunt Maud's the next day, but she goes back anyway. I feel she is put off by the incessant family ructions. Yesterday had seen a terrible scene because Eve hates her job and slammed doors. This aggravated Dad and he clouts her. She is in hysterics afterwards and Mum comforts her after work.

As usual, noisy life events are blinding me to the silence of my plural.

JAUNTS OF 1985

16 April 1985: Another Picnic at Kerb Abbot

I have instigated a picnic to Kerb Abbot. How odd. Almost exactly three years have passed since my secret picnic in Kerb Abbot with Eve and Mazie. I had suffered all manner of horrible physical and emotional symptoms.

That morning, I had picked up photos of Eve's illustrations for a plant story I had written (along with drawings of popstars and children). After a trip to Debton, I suggest this picnic with Mum, Eve, Mazie and an older sister. We go via car. I recall this picnic and didn't enjoy it much. I have come to learn my plural has begun to view the behaviours of certain family members as doorkeeping. Mazie has changed and cannot be seen as a younger me anymore; Mum wants me to move out, and (except for Eve) I'm hiding from everyone a secret world that would soon become my novel. My plural would rather I had come alone.

Of course, these family members aren't doorkeepers at all. They are just people living within their own realms. An inner confusion has occurred because I have a plural.

ROUTE 29: 26 April 1985: A Jog Down Fox Road

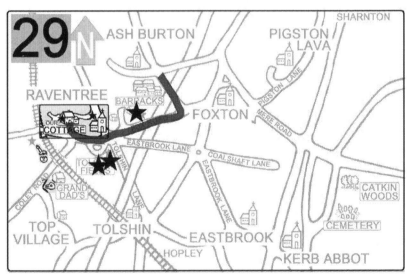

Eve, a friend and I jog down Foxton Road towards the Barracks.

I haven't been on a self-instigated jaunt to the east of the village (except for a one-off on 19 June 1983) in three years. And this hasn't been instigated by me either.

That day, I had skived from uni, writing my novel *The Lessons* on the coach home. I had begun this novel three days ago and a nasty bug had cut me down for almost a week. My symptoms are almost a carbon-copy of those surrounding my secret picnic on 5th April 1982. This is because my novel (like my picnic) has been fuelled by my toddlerhood.

On my arrival home, I found Eve and a friend had arranged to go jogging. So I came. 'Jogged past the Inn and then walked about seven miles, (I had written). Talked. Felt great. Became a bit chilly. Woke in the middle of the night with a nasty sick pain. Had to sit up for a while and it gradually went. Don't know what it was.' The following day, I begin smoking after a hiatus (Dad's rollups). I had taken up smoking on the 23rd of March. I have just started a project called Nightmare Cats at City University. I am now in my second year of my degree course and my artwork has got bigger and louder. Since Sept 1983, I have been living in digs, returning to the cottage certain weekends.

Two days after this jog, I have a vile period pain that sends me to bed at 2pm. Again, I had just encountered an assault site (a farmer's gate on Fox Road). It has shed light upon those of my body: nausea (the throat) and a nasty period pain (the vagina).

Two months later, I would do something for the first time: go on a bike ride to the east of the village alone.

ROUTE 30: 5 July 1985: The End of Nightmare Cats

I have now quit my Nightmare Cats project after a growing disenchantment with it. Nightmare Cats depict distorted cats' faces with huge yawning mouths. I felt ill the entire time I worked on these paintings. This is because they are describing sensations of oral rape.

I have just returned from a hectic weekend at Aunt Maud's (28 June – 2 July) where I had begun a brief affair with Maud's next door's son, Nate.

I was glad my second year at uni was coming to an end for feeling fraught. I'd hoped to see Eve, but she is now in a serious relationship with a work colleague, Simon. I report in my diary that I 'hate home'. The day after my bike ride, I go on a daytrip to Brittany with Eve and a friend.

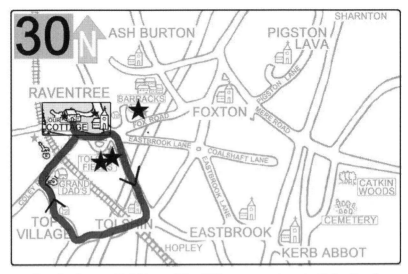

I cycle alone to Tolshin and Top Village, returning via Coley Road.

This incidence of going on bike rides after completing a creative project has occurred several times before and would happen again. On 14th June 1986, I take a lone bike ride two days after hanging my degree show. The completion of a project fuelled by my toddlerhood appears to have triggered this bike ride.

ROUTE 31: **8 July 1985: Bike Ride Revisited**

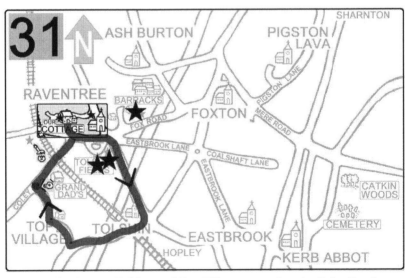

I cycle alone to Tolshin and Top Village, returning via Coley Road.

Three days after my lone bike ride, I'm repeating the same one.

While Eve and Nicholas are out with their partners, I take a ride down Tolshin Lane, ending my circuit with Coley Road where Granddad used to live. Things are bad between Mum and me. She wants me out by the summer holidays and suggest I take my paintings to Maud's. I return to uni the next day depressed. I feel Mum doesn't mean what she says. She is trapped in a terrible marriage and is upset because I have spent time at Maud's. The two of them have never got on.

ROUTE 32: 27 Sept 1985: Another Mock Assault Site

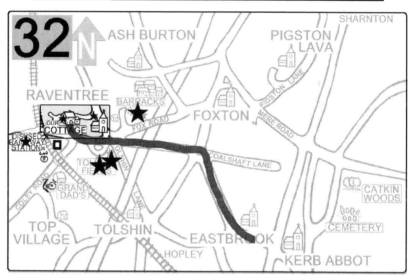

I walk with Eve to Eastbrook.

After two-and-a-half months of no jaunts, I take three in as many days.

I have just begun my third year at City Uni and (between 25 Aug and 18 Sept 1985), have been producing alfresco oil paintings of a railway bridge and cattle-gate one-bridge up from the disused railway station. A bridleway cuts across fields to this secluded spot where Dad takes the dog for a walk. A square to the left of the map marks this painting spot. As can be seen, it's not far from the broken finds of April 1978 and is just across the way from where Granddad used to live.

So, a gate again and this one is close to an assault site.

But something incredible is happening here and strongly connects to my secret bike ride of 5th April 1982.

A Gate with a Pointing Tree

As seen, my plural is constantly reminded of my toddlerhood without my conscious awareness. She wants the truth out but a doorkeeper in my head keeps hiding things from me.

Here, my plural is using existing resources to convey a message to me. She is limited by what is available. But I have just found another gate, a cattle-gate beneath a railway bridge, and it would form centre-stage for my paintings. Not only that, but my plural has found a means of pointing in a particular direction: east-north-east. The target is the Fox Road gate, where I was raped at three. She is pointing at it.

How is this possible? The answer is a dead tree. I had found one in the bushes and asked Dad to place it on the cattle-gate for me. I then shifted it this way and that to improve the composition. But sneakily, my plural was pointing this tree directly towards the Fox Road assault site on the other side of the village.

These sketches would become the theme for my degree show in July 1986. Huge gates would commandeer, and in later studio pieces, distant poplars would become vulva-shaped.

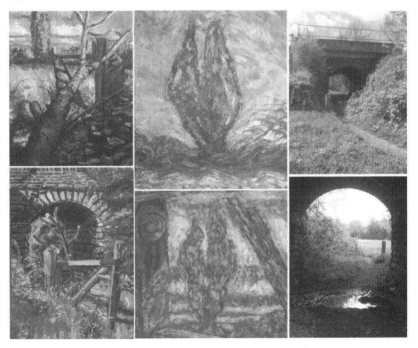

The images on the previous page shows my paintings and my sketching spot beneath this railway tunnel.

Images left: My oil sketches (Sept 1985) of the dead tree resting on the cattle-gate near a railway bridge. The upper image faces northeast, the lower image, southwest. Notice chief limbs pointing a certain way.

Central images: Sections of my degree pieces (July 1986). The poplars, taken from my sketches have become vulva-shaped.

Images right: How this painting spot looks over thirty years later. The dead tree and cattle-gate are gone. Only the post remains.

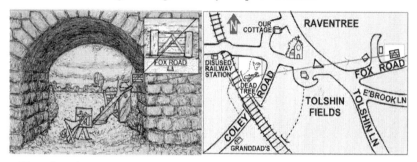

The drawings above show a reconstruction of my sketching spot beneath this railway bridge (not to be confused with the railway bridge in Tolshin Fields further up the line). The map on the right shows the aerial map view. Although not to scale, the angles are accurate. The tree is pointing from one gate to another.

Studio pieces taken from these early sketches (mid-Nineties).

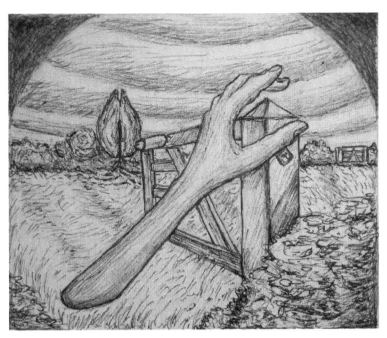

The Pointing Tree

The image shows the true meaning beneath my oil sketches. The tree is really a pointer, like a hand, indicating east-north-east, and the gate is the target (another gate, concealed from this spot). The poplars would become vulva-shaped in my degree pieces and the gate's bracket would take on the actions of a phallus impaling the vulva. The vulva appears to bleed into the cornfield. The ripples in the clouds and corn represent the aftershock of trauma.

I had produced my oil sketches beneath the railway bridge close to the disused railway station and the tree is pointing to another assault site. Interestingly, half the cattle-gate slats are missing. I liked the ruined look and retained the appearance. But it's like my missing plural and the reason I would fail to see this message for thirty-five years. I suffered chronic depression and grief feelings whilst working towards my degree show.

Charcoal Sketches

So, my degree work is just beginning and all would tell on my toddlerhood. I would open my project with charcoal sketches from my alfresco paintings. These sketches are distorted interpretations of the graffitied railway bridge. I wanted to convey a threatening atmosphere like the climactic scene of my novel, *The Lessons*. The setting of this novel is in fact the disused railway station itself and surreptitiously describes my rape there.

That weekend, Eve and I take three walks to the east of the village beginning with the one to Eastbrook described here. I report the walk was 'nice'. We go nowhere near an assault site, but the following day, we would walk right past the farmer's gate on Fox Road.

After rendering my charcoal sketches, I coach home to learn Nate has had a nervous breakdown. He has finished a long-term relationship and I wondered if my name had been mentioned. I'd had a hectic month at Maud's (between 19 July – 14 Aug) and hoped I had lost my virginity to him on the 8th of Aug. I am confused I had lost no blood after intercourse like Eve had. I go to the doctor's about it the following January. I am told my hymen was already broken.

Things don't progress between Nate and me. Again, I can't seem to sustain a boyfriend and the whole affair leaves me unsettled.

Things are still bad between Mum and me. She wants to move into my bedroom now and creates friction with Mazie. I hate the idea and we row. I feel now that she was trying to drive me out. I think she had her suspicions about her half-brother and couldn't bear the thought.

ROUTE 33: 28 Sept 1985: Going the Keep Out Way

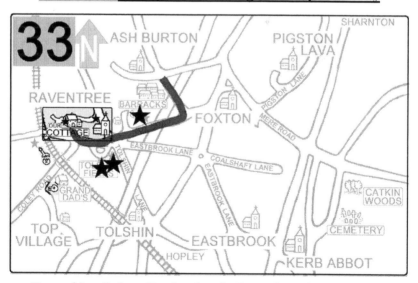

Eve and I walk down Fox Road to the Barracks and have a picnic.

65

The next day, Eve and I take a walk to the Barracks and have a picnic. I would have strolled right past the Fox Road gate. Did I glance that way? I'll never know, but I wrote in my diary, 'Found a spot by a deserted road and ate our sandwiches. I wore a headband.' I notice I wore this same headband during my degree show the following July. It's in my photos. It's black. Black, as in black-out. Or coma. Oblivion. I am oblivious.

Here, I appear drawn to the 'keep out' signs after making the (subconscious) decision to centre my degree show upon an assault site. Later that day, Eve and I visit June Cox and her fiancé in their new flat.

ROUTE 34: 29 Sept 1985: Mocks and Projections

Eve and I walk to Tolshin and Top Village, returning via Coley Road.

A day has passed since my Barracks picnic. Things are terrible at home. I see less of Eve as she is moving on with Simon and it also become obvious that Mazie isn't a younger me at all. In fact, she is the opposite: outgoing and having boyfriends. This is a lesson I needed to learn, but sadly my oblivion would prevail and so would my confusion. For years to come, I would project my younger self upon internalised children, such as nieces and nephews, wishing my toddlerhood was like theirs.

Today Eve and I go on a long walk down Tolshin Lane and finish off at Coley Road. Meanwhile, my toddlerhood traumas are fuelling my degree show. Never would I see how this connected to a secret picnic on 5th April 1982. And that all goes back to my rape in toddlerhood.

JAUNTS OF 1986

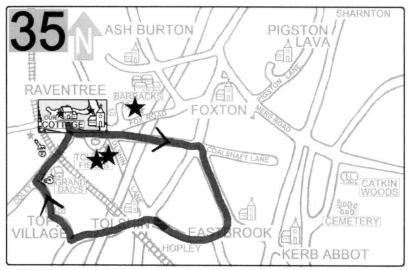

I cycle alone to Eastbrook, Hopley, Tolshin and Top Village, returning via Coley Road.

On 5th April, Nan has moved in with us. Aunt Maud can't look after her anymore and things are frostier than ever between Mum and Maud. Today, I go on a bike ride on my own.

I report of a lovely bike ride if the gear wasn't stiff. I've hung my degree show two days ago and huge gates and bleeding vulvas (disguised as poplars) abound within my art space.

In two days' time, I will begin my second draft of *The Lessons* after fifteen months of writing little. I'm messing with a piano Mum has just bought and would play old tunes (badly). We used to have a piano in the early Seventies and (with Nan living with us) the cottage feels closer to my toddlerhood. The day after this bike ride, I show Eve a derelict house at the top of our lane called The Stables. A derelict house features within my novel. It is called The Hollows at Elmhurst Station. It is a creepy old place with a sunken roof and decaying Sixties décor. I am in fact describing the abandoned cottage of my toddlerhood.

The main character of my novel is called Aidan. My rapist's name hides within this name.

ROUTE 36: **29 June 1986: Home from Uni**

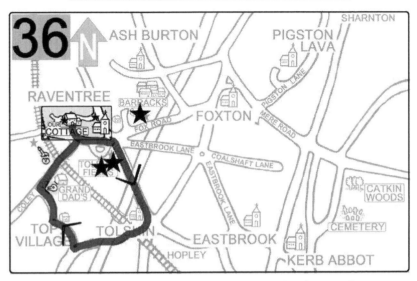

I walk alone to Tolshin, Top Village and Coley Road.

I have completed my degree course at uni and would soon learn I had almost failed due to my appalling dissertation. Still, I am pleased to have earned an upper-second with honours due to the strength of my paintings. I am glad to return home after a difficult three years. I'm now feverishly reading books on how-to write novels and am still working on my second draft of *The Lessons*.

I report of a six-mile walk beginning with Tolshin Lane and ending with Coley Road. I believe this walk was triggered by completing my degree course.

The Tumbledown Barn Mock Assault Site

In mid-October 1986, I go on three jaunts in five days. I am now a postgraduate on the dole and living at the cottage. Per fortnight, I'm signing on in Debton, traversable via the disused railway station. Between 27 July and 21 Sept 1986, I would produce alfresco oils of a tumbledown barn in a barley field. More alfresco paintings, it seems and this one is situated to the north of the cottage.

On 9th Aug 1986, I report of having a bike ride but I don't say where. Throughout the summer, I suffered inexplicable periods pains and cramps. Without realising, I had mocked-up yet another rape site and it is spurring

68

physical symptoms again. On the 27th of July, I had placed a plank in the doorway of this barn. The intention was to break up the sky. Instead, I had given an unsavoury slant to the composition.

To the northeast of the barn is a broken gate. On 7th Sept I had written in my diary, 'Did three small paintings. I felt they had uncovered secrets. They were studies of light on the heads of barley, the broken gate and sky.' Throughout the autumn, I would produce studio copies of these paintings in the workshop.

This broken gate stands to the northeast of the barn. The coordinates echo that of the actual cottage and the Fox Road gate. The barn is like a ghost of my childhood cottage and where my toddlerhood has been lost. Sometimes, I had odd notions of an old fireplace, a stove or armchairs within those walls, but has since been worn away.

Images left: Paintings of the tumbledown barn and broken gate in July 1986. I had placed a plank across the barn doorway to improve the composition. Not realising, I had created a rape symbol.

Images right: Photo of the barn in Feb 1987. The map lower right shows the location of the barn in relation to the cottage. The barn has come to represent my cottage abandoned and where I was raped. Along with my toddlerhood, it stand neglected and falls into dereliction.

69

Where Nan Lives

A further complication is Nan – my rapist's mother.

On 8th Sept 1986, she has moved into sheltered accommodation on the other side of the village. By now, she had lived with us for five months. Her complex is just round the corner from two assault sites: Tolshin Lane and Tolshin Fields. How appalling. I would regularly walk to Nan's via a little lane skirting these Fields. I had barely seen Tolshin Fields since 11th May 1980 when Dad, Eve and I had traversed them. I am now regularly seeing them from the roadside.

ROUTE 37: **12 Oct 1986: Where Nan Lives**

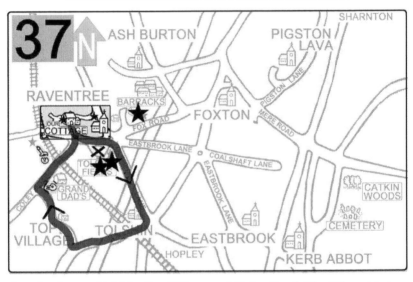

I cycle alone to Tolshin, Top Village and Coley Road. The 'X' next to two assault sites marks the location of Nan's complex.

My final jaunt to the barn that year was 5th October 1986. Dad has now tarted up the workshop at the back of the cottage so I can produce copies of these barn paintings. The workshop is cold and leaky but I have a paraffin heater and am able to retreat there when things get fraught in the house.

'Felt awful and sleepy this morning,' (I had written). I then report of my lone bike ride beginning with Tolshin Lane. I have almost finished some snow sketches and am about to begin studio copies of the barn.

Nan comes round that day and I go to a local club with Dad. That evening, I'm writing my novel but writer's block hampers my progress.

The next day, I would walk to Nan's and then go to bingo that evening with Mum at the complex.

As seen here, I am surrounded with reminders of my toddlerhood.

ROUTE 38: **14 Oct 1986: Tolshin Fields Returning**

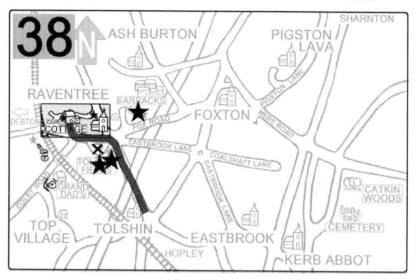

Eve and I walk down Tolshin Lane and back.

Today is foggy and I meet Eve at Debton Library. We then walk down Tolshin Lane. I feel like the gooseberry of the house, as everyone seems to have a life but me. My relationship with Mark keeps floundering as I had lived away from home for long periods, but again, suspect my inability to have a boyfriend is the real reason.

The previous day, I had walked to Nan's complex again via the lane skirting Tolshin Fields and would do the same thing on the 15th and the 16th. I keep seeing Tolshin Fields' scrublands where I was raped eighteen years ago.

I'm now working on a copy of the front view of the barn including a close up of the plank slashing through. 'Hated doing it,' (I had written). I cried on completing this painting. My appetite is bad and my depression is chronic. On the 15th, I mention suicide in my diary.

ROUTE 39: **17 Oct 1986: The Final Jaunt**

The day begins with a driving lesson but my diary doesn't say where. I'd been having driving lessons since 25th June 1982 and my progress is slow.

I am about to fail my test for the second time. I then walk to Debton to meet Eve (via the disused railway station). I visit Nan for the fifth time in six days. My exposure to Tolshin Fields continues. Eve and I then walk down Eastbrook Lane.

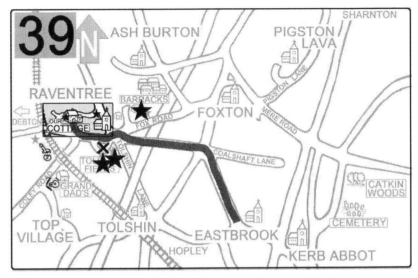

Eve and I walk down Eastbrook Lane and back.

'I'm depressed,' (I had written). After a spell of terrible writer's block, I report my burning fantasy world has renewed force. For years to come, I would struggle with my novel, *The Lessons*, and not know the fuel.

No more jaunts to the east of the village are reported in my diaries. Both Nan's death and my move-out into a bedsit in May 1987 would put a lid on things. But until then, I was walking past Tolshin Fields regularly when visiting Nan.

In October 1987, I would marry the art student I had met in May 1983, Mark. He had triggered me into including Krakatoa in my weather project, for his semblance to Uncle Dan.

My relationship with Mark is about to pick up after months of vacillating. In May 1987, we would get engaged and we would marry in the October.

My relationship with Mark tells me a lot about my toddlerhood. In April 1987, he would visit the cottage for the first time.

4. Jaunts and Boyfriends
(May 1987 – June 1993)

My behaviour on Mark's maiden visits to the village sheds further light upon the location of these assault sites. As seen, Mark bore semblance to my uncle in 1968, being tall, broad and dark with (occasional) facial hair. Throughout my courtship and marriage to him, a burning fantasy world had consumed me. This (and other symptoms) seems to have been triggered by these semblances. The following describes the leadup to his maiden visits to the cottage and what happens.

May-June 1983: Meeting Mark and the Krakatoa Effect

On 10th May 1983, I first meet Mark. He would say hello to me on the 11th. That day, I have upset stomach, headache, sore throat and suffer bouts of vertigo. Since 28th Feb 1982, I had been working on a weather project (superseding earlier ones). I'm writing about hurricanes, tornadoes and lightning. Soon after meeting Mark, I would insert volcanoes and tsunamis into my weather project. I would then select a scorched theme for my mock A level and do a still life on toys.

Eve would sometimes tease me about Mark and include him in our silly stories and creepy-John drawings that would eventually become my novel. This spurs trapped feelings of my toddlerhood. My subconscious is having unwanted notions of my uncle when I encounter Mark and these notions are creating symptoms and leaking out in my behaviour.

Mark's Maiden Visits to the Village

So Mark's physique has proved to be triggering me without my realisation. Fast forward to spring 1987 and Mark visits the cottage for the first time. This is what happens.

On 20th April 1987, Mark makes his first visit. The cottage was looking shabby and I was uptight. Where did I take him? The lane skirting Tolshin scrublands close to Nan's. Although not mentioned in my diary, I recall chatting as we overlooked the scrublands. We didn't go to Nan's and Mark never met him, so why did I take him there? We then had a drink in the Weavers, a pub close to Fox Road. The logical route to this pub is Tolshin Lane – another assault site.

Mark then stops the night after spending time in my room. Mum insists he sleep in the next room, where Uncle Dan had slept over Christmas

1968. I felt odd about Mark being there, something familiar about the setting but I couldn't imagine how. This is because a doorkeeper in my head is preventing me from seeing a similar big man entering the bedroom of my toddlerhood.

The next day (21st April 1987), I walk Mark to Debton via the disused railway station. (In a fortnight, I would move into a bedsit just outside this town). Until this time, there was no reason to take Mark over this bridge.

Mark continues to visit the cottage in June and early July. During this time, I would paint his portrait in the cottage workshop surrounded with my barn and bridge paintings. I would then take him to the derelict Stables. I had already been there a few times in April 1983 and got a little obsessed about it.

Finally on 21st August 1987, I took Mark to Privy Woods. 'Haven't been there since school,' (I had written in my diary) which makes it ten years. I came over all 'stifled' and 'wanted to get away from him.' I don't remember this at all. Did I really feel this way? I think back to my memory of being ferried across the recreation grounds to these woods one cloudy day in my pushchair by Uncle Dan.

Reminders of Another Place

Mark's initial visits to the cottage included an intensive spell of showing him the assault sites of my toddlerhood (including the cottage itself): Tolshin scrublands, Tolshin Lane, Fox Road (in a pub close by) and the disused railway station. Later, I would take him to Privy Woods, then show him a 'broken home'.

During our ensuing months together, we walked everywhere as we had little money and no car. We traversed over railway bridges, through woods, scrublands, fields and lanes. I now realise I am being reminded of assault sites as I walk beside a man who evokes notions of my toddlerhood.

Visits to The Tumbledown Barn

On the 4th and 23rd February 1988 (after beginning a photography course), I would take Mark to the tumbledown barn where I had produced oil sketches in the summer of 1986. By placing a plank across the doorway, I had created a mock assault site. In 1987, Mark and I would attend a photography course and I would choose the barn as my subject matter.

I am showing Mark another broken home.

Living With Mark

In May 1988, Mark and I would get a flat together. We lived in a rural outcrop of Nilworth. His parents lived two miles down the road and we often used to walk up. This road strongly resembles the Kerb Abbot lane of my secret picnic (the one with the cemetery and Catkin Woods). No cemetery exists on this lane, but its name contains 'bury'.

After a while, I got notions of a hollow man waiting for me on a corner. He was like a ghost that became visible in misty weather when the damp revealed his form. I considered writing about him but never did.

The bike rides of my childhood are now a distant memory yet I continue to be surrounded with echoes of the past. The 'bury' road had a few hedges and farmer's gates dotted along the way; another road curved eastwards in a similar fashion to Fox Road.

Woodlands overshadow Mark's parents' house. Clearings abound as well as undergrowth. A small ruin can be found to the north of these woods. I am being reminded of Privy Woods again. Everywhere I go, I am being reminded of assaults sites of my toddlerhood.

Throughout my marriage to Mark, I was feverishly writing my novel. Little did I realise, I was providing a voice for my plural. She was telling me about the disused railway station while I thought the place was fictional. Sore throats and head-colds would gather momentum along with intrusive thoughts and depression. No wonder. I was living with a tall, broad man that provided my plural unsavoury comparisons with a rapist who shared my toddlerhood home.

A New Life

My marriage to Mark would end in July 1992 and I would move back to the cottage. In September 1993, I met my present partner, Paul. Sadly, I would repeat my odd behaviour with him too, showing him the assault sites of my toddlerhood. By then, I had quit my diary five years ago but I clearly recall walking him across Tolshin Fields. Incredibly, rapeseed was growing there at the time. I hadn't stepped foot in these fields since Dad took Eve and me on 11th May 1980. Afterwards, I would take Paul to the Inn Pub. In front of this pub is the conspicuous sign, 'Fox Road'. The Weavers is almost directly opposite this pub.

In later years, I would look out for tumbledown buildings and derelictions and conduct a few oil sketches in Paul's presence.

Paul is tall, but similarities end there.

5. **Driving Lessons**
(25 June 1982 – 26 April 1988)

This book's final section takes a brief look at my driving lessons. They appear to echo my findings so far.

My driving lessons began slowly. I had only six in 1982. I would then have twelve in 1983, ending abruptly in the July. I had none at all in 1984 and only one in 1985. I wouldn't have regular lessons until the turn of 1986 when I was at uni and paid for them myself with my grant. I would pass my test on 26th April 1988 on my third attempt. I was twenty-two.

I am astonished I had taken so long to pass my test: almost six years. This is because I was an art student for most of this time period and clues to my toddlerhood were leaching through. My life is crammed with evocations of my toddlerhood.

I now realise I was hampered by PTSD. My plural knew the cause and I didn't. Having two views of the world isn't helping my concentration either.

At first, these lessons took place to the east of the village; later they would occur in the City when I was at Uni and then in Nilworth after my graduation.

These early lessons of course are of interest. But driving down a road lacks the immediacy of cycling or walking down it; landmarks and road signs can pass unnoticed. However, this strand of my life is revealing and this is what I have found.

Driving Lessons of 1982

25 June 1982 (Friday evening): A drive through Foxton and the Barracks

This would be my first driving lesson and I have just turned seventeen.

I haven't been down these lanes since my bike ride of 16th April 1982 (on encountering Catkin Woods in cloudy weather and a woman had reprimanded me). After a day at college, I am instructed to drive through Foxton and the Barracks. I would drive past an assault site and the 'keep out' signs. These landmarks may have whizzed past without my notice, but my subconscious would have known they were there.

The day after this drive, I report of feeling very depressed. I wrote in my diary, 'cried a lot in the afternoon and evening because I am so disappointed in myself.' Eve and I are decorating our bedroom and that night, I suffer unexplained nausea. Other triggers are in force here so I do not believe the driving lesson alone had caused these responses.

I have five more driving lessons that year and most are to the east of the village. The final one would be late autumn as described here.

20 Nov 1982 (Saturday morning): Route unknown

'Felt terrible in my driving lesson,' (I had written). I have been suffering aching joints, nausea crampy stomach and a head-cold since the 17th. These illnesses are due to my copious artwork at college. I jogged round the garden to clear my head. It didn't work. I'm drawing hurricane tracks for my weather project.

Driving Lessons of 1983

After a slow start, my driving lessons pick up again. Eve doesn't have any for a while after she has corrective surgery to hide a scar on her check (3rd Jan) and the wound scabs over.

8 Jan 1983 (Sat morn): Eastbrook, Foxton and a road to Nilworth

Nan is stopping with us. I report of the sky during the drive: 'A lovely sunrise, clear. I could see transparent bands of clouds. Almost an illusion.' The next day, I'm sorting my weather notes and photocopying images of tornadoes. Later, there is a terrible scene between Mum and Dad.

I remember this drive, for the striking sky. I was travelling northeast, towards the something-over-there feeling. I felt I was journeying into another place but I could never reach it.

Between January and July, I have ten further driving lessons but am no longer reporting the routes. During this time, I am producing a lot of artwork informing upon my toddlerhood, such as big cats and toys. My tornado project is ongoing.

The following is worthy of note.

6 July 1983: (Wed afternoon): Route Unknown

I describe my lesson as 'hectic. I seem to do everything wrong. When I turn right I don't keep parallel with the line in the middle of the road. Instead I go beyond it.' My instructor gives me an eye-test afterwards.

The previous day is relevant.

On 5th July I went to college to pick up my artwork to find a love letter from Mark. (On the 4th, we'd had our first date and I was 'screwed with nerves'). The letter triggered inexplicable trapped feelings inside. I wrote back and two days later, Mark would reply, apologising for his heavy letter. I would pack my stuff for a stay at Aunt Maud's for a month. Eve and I would return on the 24ᵗʰ and I wouldn't have another driving lesson for almost two years.

My terrible driving lesson appears due to my trapped feelings of the previous day. These feelings are from my toddlerhood.

Driving Lessons of 1984 – 1988

Between May 1984 and July 1986, I have driving lessons in the City whilst I was at uni. My first one (on 21 May 1985) was 'disastrous' and I am put off until Jan 1986. This bad opening lesson might be due to my previous lessons, always being to the east of the village thus far. My artwork has also got big and loud and I am often feeling under the weather. I would fail my test on 22ⁿᵈ May 1986.

From July to Nov 1986, my driving lessons would take place in my hometown, but I am no longer going to the east of the village, or driving passing assault sites. Instead, I am regularly exposed to Tolshin Fields because of where Nan lives. I am walking past an assault site prior to these lessons.

I would fail my test again on 3ʳᵈ Nov 1986 and refrain from further lessons for eighteen months.

Exposure to these assault sites appears to be hampering my progress in my driving ability. Large gaps occur between bouts and I keep making silly mistakes. Examples are the trapped feelings of my toddlerhood in June 1983 when I began my lessons. I would then pass doorkeeper signs and can't concentrate. My copious artwork fuelled by my toddlerhood would further hamper me, as well as visits to Nan's complex in the latter part of 1986. I am regularly exposed to Tolshin Fields from the roadside.

My driving lessons then stall for eighteen months. Initially, this was due to having no money.

I would resume my driving lessons on 11ᵗʰ March 1988 shortly before moving into a flat with Mark. I am no longer exposed to assault sites on my routes and I haven't driven to the east of the village since July 1983.

I finally pass my test on 26ᵗʰ April 1988 after almost six years of driving lessons.

6. Conclusion

During the time period covered in this book, I was completely oblivious to the truth about my toddlerhood. I didn't know I had a plural and I didn't know about these assault sites. Least of all, I didn't know a hidden part of me has been making unsavoury associations with landmarks and placenames due to a vile toddlerhood.

The clues within my diaries, artwork, stories, physical and emotional symptoms has told me a lot about my toddlerhood, and this includes the location of assault sites. But care is needed not to confuse these with mock ones. I have learned to be mindful of echoes. This means going back in time to the beginning. This means looking out for my plural's voice within my creations.

One thing I can never be certain of, is whether Uncle Dan took me somewhere else. Are other assault sites waiting to be discovered? What else did he do? Sadly, the toddler brain cannot process information like that of an older self. She can never testify in a way that can be used as evidence. Uncle Dan exploited this to his advantage. Had I never kept a diary, or expressed myself in various ways, I would have continued to explain my problems to the wrong things and oblivion would have prevailed for the rest of my life.

The aim of this book it to shed light upon the mind of the abused toddler and the strange phenomena of the plural. Perhaps one day, these findings can be used to help others.

Oil sketches conducted in the early Nineties. Notice the house sliced through by a tree in the composition. I was unaware of what I had done until late in the painting. The painting on the right shows a split cornfield leading to a split house. My artwork continues to divulge of the split self.

Other Books by the Author

Image: My jaunt in September 2020 looking towards Top Village. Tolshin Fields is behind me.

Tales from Daler Cottage: Unearthing the Hidden Codes within my Children's Mysteries

Mirror Image Shattered: A Twin's True Story

The Locked Door: The Hidden Novel Behind the Kidnap Thriller

The Lessons: The True Story of a Parasitic Novel

North Window: The Stranger behind the Reflection

Nadia: Testament of the Ghost Girl

Blood in Water: Eight Short Stories

Blood on the Corn: Uncovering the Assault Sites of my Toddlerhood

The author lives in the UK and writes under a pseudonym.

Understanding Old Photographs

by

ROBERT POLS

Robert Boyd
PUBLICATIONS

Published by
Robert Boyd Publications
260 Colwell Drive
Witney, Oxfordshire OX8 7LW

First published 1995

ISBN: 1-899536-01-9

Printed and bound at The Alden Press, Oxford

Contents

Cover illustration: Cabinet Print; Hop Sing & Co., Calcutta

Introduction   5

Chapter 1 Evoking the Experience   7
  The Extremes   7
  The Studio   8
  The Photographer   12
  Suggestions for Dress   16
  Posing the Sitter   17
  The Ordeal   19
  Photographing Children   23
  Prices and Services   26

Chapter 2 Appreciating the Artefact   28
  Flyleaves   30
  Lost Colour   31
  Added Colour   33
  Three Kinds of Popularity   34

Chapter 3 Interpreting the Image – Portraits   38
  Personality   38
  Class   41
  Character   44
  Family   47
  Contrasts   55
  Stereotypes   59
  When the Smiling Starts   59

Contents continued

Chapter 4 Interpreting the Image – Occasions and Events   63
  Family Occasions   66
  Work and Play   69
  Institutional Pictures   70
  Public Events   72
  Dressing Up   75

Bibliography   80

General Index   82

Index of Photographers and Photographic Suppliers   85

ACKNOWLEDGEMENT

The author is grateful to C. R. Stevenson for permission to reproduce a number of photographs from his collection.

Introduction

A *Punch* cartoon of 6th January 1883 shows a butcher standing proud and aproned, one hand on hip, the other on generous stomach, outside a shop festooned with plucked, hanging turkeys and the occasional pig. A small crowd is gathering to watch him being photographed. The caption, economic with risibility, reads, 'The Festive Season – A Proud Moment'. The cartoon shows that the Victorians had embraced the infant art enthusiastically and were ever anxious to be photographed. Indeed, this is just one of a long line of *Punch* cartoons attesting to their appetite. Queen Victoria filled well over a hundred family albums, and where the queen went, her subjects followed. But the cartoon also draws attention to the fact that photography can make a statement. The picture being taken is not just a portrait of a man: it will tell the world that the subject has made a success of life and takes a pride in being something big in poultry. Thus the cartoon depicts a process of conscious image-making.

There are perhaps two main aspects to the image made by a photograph: it can provide a record and it can make a statement.

The idea of photography as a record was apparent from its very beginnings. Henry Fox Talbot, the pioneer of photography, wondered, 'What would not be the value to the English Nobility of such a record of their ancestors?' That value was quickly recognised, not just by the nobility but by the population as a whole, and that recognition earns the gratitude of family historians today. The attractions of portraiture were, of course, apparent long before the invention of photography. Pliny, in the first century, claimed that the very earliest likeness was made by a girl who traced the outline of her lover's shadow on a wall, the better to remember him in his absence. But it was photography that brought portraiture into every home, satisfying our impulse to record loved ones (and ourselves) before age does its worst and death or geography takes them away. Photography-as-record can also put people in a context, stimulating memory and providing proof of activities, events and family milestones.

The notion that photography can make a statement was also expressed early in its history. Lady Eastlake, in 1855, described it as 'a new form of communications between man and man'. It has a symbolic function, projecting a view of the sitter as a member of family, social group or society. That view may be the sitter's or it may speak of the photographer's assumptions. In either case, it may very well be the kind of view taken generally at the time.

This book sets out to consider photographic image-making in the years before the First World War, with reference particularly to the kinds of picture passed down through the family. The basic concerns of identification and dating have been considered in an earlier book, *Dating Old Photographs*. This one is more concerned with understanding the photos that we have inherited, looking at the actual business of making the image, at the image as an object we now hold in our hands, and at some of the sorts of subjects and statements that the image may deal with.

It has often been argued that family history is directed not just at establishing a skeleton outline of descent, but at putting flesh on its bones. In a similar way, this book aims to encourage a filling out of photography's bony basics of 'What is it?', 'Who is it?', and 'When was it?'.

In the course of making its points, the text will refer to or describe more photographs than are included as illustrations. Some of those mentioned are now too faded for satisfactory reproduction; others are excluded with the aim of keeping illustrations to a manageable number. It is hoped that descriptions of a wider range of pictures will usefully supplement those examples which are actually shown.

1. *Evoking the Experience*

One day in August 1992 our family of three went into a photographer's, were taken into a curtained room with subdued lights, arranged in a series of standing and sitting permutations and photographed, by flash and fill-in lighting, some dozen times. We then went off to do some shopping and have coffee, before returning an hour later to view the results. The photographs were as successful as they could possibly be, which is to say that each of us observed, 'Well, they're very good of you two.' We bought a selection of shots, each card-mounted. The whole occasion had been relaxed, quick and painless. It was not ever thus...

The Extremes

On 23rd March 1841, at the Royal Polytechnic Institution, Richard Beard opened what was the first public photographic studio in Britain and, possibly, in Europe. The reasonably moneyed classes flocked to his door. Once inside, they found themselves in splendid reception rooms which were designed to impress. Grandeur was the order of the day in the more aspiring studios, and another early professional, Antoine Claudet, was to refer to his Regent Street premises as a 'temple to photography'.

Changing rooms were provided, and maids were at hand to help. Suitable clothes were also available, and both Beard and John Mayall, another up-market practitioner soon to appear on the scene, tried to persuade clients to wear garments from the studio's wardrobe. This was to prove unpopular, and photographers in general quickly settled for just offering clients advice on how to dress for the occasion. Sitters then submitted to having their faces made up before being conducted to the circular studio on the roof.

In the centre of the studio, raised on a platform, was a revolving chair, which could be turned to catch the light filtering through the blue glass windows in the ceiling. Blue glass had been chosen to reduce glare and diffuse the light without increasing the exposure time. The client ascended the steps to the platform, sat in the chair, and had the head held by a clamp to keep it still during the exposure, which took between 1½ and 3 minutes according to the light conditions.

The eventual result, a 4x6cm daguerrotype framed in a velvet-lined morocco case, cost one guinea, or two if hand-coloured. Portraits of two or three people together were rather more expensive, since the more people there were posing, the greater chance there was of one moving and causing the first attempt to fail. It might in passing be noted that the world was well-stocked with people for whom a guinea represented more than a week's income. But photography was quickly to become possible for all levels of society.

The 1861 edition of Mayhew's *Life and Labour of the London Poor* includes a description of a Bermondsey street photographer. In a furniture broker's yard Mr F. had erected in front of his showman's caravan a booth built up of old canvas cloths, originally used in the fairground. These were spread over a makeshift frame of posts and clothes-horses, and, to let light into the 'studio', a glazed roof had been contrived from two old windows. Outside the booth was a crowd of people examining pinned-up samples of Mr F.'s work, whilst inside a queue of women and children waited their turn. It was Mrs F. who actually operated the camera, for, as her husband explained, 'People prefers more to be took by a woman than a man... It's quite natural, for a lady don't mind taking her bonnet off and tucking up her hair, or sticking a pin in here or there before one of her own sect, which before a man proves objectionable.' Once exposed, the tiny glass plate, 'scarcely larger than a visiting card', was taken by a youth to Mr F., who was waiting in the caravan to carry out the processing. The resulting portraits, apparently cartes de visite, were drab images of stiff, nervous figures against a nondescript pale background.

Mayhew went on to visit another studio, this time a converted shop, outside which a front-man attempted to drum up custom. Presumably because the shop itself was too dark, pictures were taken in the adjoining alley, where a blanket had been hung up as a backdrop. Though open to the sky, the alley was very gloomy and the sixpenny result (or eightpenny result, if the customer was sufficiently gullible) was almost black. The only detail Mayhew could make out was 'a slight light on one side of the face'. That this was a tintype is suggested by the darkness of the image and by the fact that a departing customer thought it worth trying to polish it on his cuff in an attempt to make it brighter.

Most would-be photographees went, of course, to premises somewhere between the two extremes, and any one studio differed not only from others, but also in its own practices over a period of years. Such variability should be borne in mind when reading the notes on the photographic experience which make up this chapter.

The Studio

Photographic businesses proliferated in Victorian Britain. Small country towns had several and the big cities many. At one point there were thirty-five studios in Regent Street alone.

The exterior of a studio commonly incorporated a shop front with its windows full of photographs: portraits in various sizes, local and more exotic views, in which there was a brisk trade, and stereo cards.

A carte of the London and Chester Photographic Company carries on the back a picture of their premises (*see figure 1*). The ground floor is, indeed, a photo-filled shop front, with a lady looking in the window. A gentleman is entering the building, while an open carriage waits outside. The frontage of the second floor is given over almost entirely to windows, and the third floor is recessed to allow a large expanse of the floor below to be glass-roofed. Clearly the main taking of pictures was carried out on the second floor. A man is standing on the upper (third floor) roof, to which an open door shows easy access. This suggests a further location that could

Figure 1. Carte de visite; London & Chester Photo. Co., Chester.

be readily put to use, either for securing or for processing photographs. The face of the building is liberally furnished with advertising messages, including 'Portrait Rooms', 'Picture Frame Manufacturer' and the name of the firm.

Once inside the door the customers found themselves in a reception area which, particularly in the more aspiring establishments, was very imposing. This space doubled as a display area where examples of the photographer's art, especially portraits of the better class of patron, could be examined. Leading from it was often a ladies' dressing room or parlour. The décor of the reception rooms was as plush as the firm could run to, with oriental carpets, plaster busts and the like conveying a solid impression of the firm's standing. John Moffat's Edinburgh reception area of 1876 was described as an 'elegant apartment', and Matthew Brady's Broadway studio in New York boasted bright, patterned, velvet carpets, satin and gold wallpaper, frescoed ceiling, chandelier, rosewood furniture and a profusion of mirrors.

It will be noticed that, here and elsewhere, evidence is drawn on from outside Britain, and especially from the United States. There were, of course, differences between countries, just as there were differences within a country. America, for example, took the lead in early documentary photography, and France was the original home of the daguerrotype and the carte de visite. But photography had an international aspect and influences were mutual. German materials were used worldwide, processes were quickly taken up in new countries, and George Eastman, when he encountered problems in his development of Kodak technology, twice visited England to seek and find solutions. In studio portraiture in particular there seems to have been great commonality of practice. The clothes worn by a sitter in France or Hawaii may sometimes look different from those worn by a subject in Britain, but professional arrangements and approaches seem remarkably similar.

Eventually the sitter reached the studio where the actual operation was carried out. Contemporary illustrations generally show a high, well-lit room, with sloping glazed roof meeting a generously-windowed wall. To one end of the room a selection of backcloths and curtains hang over an area of floor which is carpeted, tiled or flagged. There are assorted items of furniture, head clamps, mirrors, a camera on a very solid stand, a photographer and a client or two.

Lighting was of paramount importance. For the first forty years or so of its life photography had to depend on daylight. So vital was this, both to the taking and to the processing of pictures, that A. H. Fry of the Royal Pavilion Studios, Brighton, headed his trade plate with a quotation from *King John*: 'The glorious sun stays in his course and plays the alchemist.'

To catch as much light as possible, studios in London were often on the roof, whilst in the provinces they were more likely to be in the back garden. Light entered from above as well as from the sides, and the extensively glazed studios were often referred to as glasshouses. Lighting from the north was often preferred, since direct sunlight could be harsh in its effect and uncomfortable for the sitters. Opening hours were shorter in winter or during foggy weather. Curtains were arranged over wall and ceiling windows and often worked, one to a pane, on the principle of blinds, each capable of being raised or lowered individually, to allow a wide range of permutations in the attempt to control and diffuse the light. Mirrors were commonly used to act as reflectors. It was not until the 1880s that electric lighting was widely introduced, and that sittings in the evening or on cloudy days became possible. This also allowed some choice in the location of the studio. By the mid-eighties Mr Boak of Bridlington was able to make capital of the fact that his studio was on the ground floor. Nevertheless, some photographers remained keen to take their pictures by natural light whenever they could.

Choice of furnishings for the studio was of some moment. Edward M. Estabrooke's 1872 list of recommendations for American Glass or Operating Rooms includes backgrounds, camera stands, copying stand, curtain, ottomans, reflectors, head rests, head cloths, curtain stand, table, table cover and posing chair. He recommends a chair 'of the most graceful design and finish', and is much impressed by Sarony's Universal Rest and Posing Chair, which was introduced in 1866. His publishers, however, do not omit to slip in, at the back of his book, an advertisement for their own product, the Gatchel and Hyatt Double Backed Chair, 'which contains all the variety, elegance and convenience that can be desired. With the short back, it admits of all changes and variety of positions to be found in any chair.... The changes are made in a moment, and the Chair is always firm and rigid.' The chair costs $25 or $28, depending on upholstery fabric, though the firm also offers a Sliding-Back Chair at half the price. A table is regarded by Gatchel and Hyatt as 'a beautiful article to fill out a picture, and to give a great many graceful positions that cannot be obtained without it.' Estabrooke believes that 'a handsome black walnut table with ornamented top produces a very nice effect', and also holds that one with a white marble top is 'conspicuously agreeable'. A cover is suggested for draping over chair or table and for arranging in such a way as to hide the foot of the headrest. After praising the versatility of ottomans or hassocks in aiding the composition of groups and the posing of children, Estabrooke reminds his readers that taste should be exercised, since the patron 'wants a likeness, and not a picture of tables, chairs, flower-pots, busts, etc., etc., *ad nauseam.*'

The most obvious piece of studio furnishing in many photographs is the backcloth. Claudet's establishment, in 1842, was the first to use painted backgrounds, and the practice grew, with changes in fashions of favoured scenes over the years, and with photographers building up a choice of stately interiors, sylvan glades, book-lined studies and the like. On occasion it may be possible to identify the scene on a backdrop: Joseph Willey, a Lincolnshire photographer, used an interior scene through the window of which could be seen the spire of Louth church. The unusual was always possible, and Gatchel and Hyatt produced scenes to order at $15 for a background measuring 8'x10'. An alternative to commissioning a scene was to make one's own, an undertaking well within the abilities of those photographers whose early training was as painters. For those who required something more simple and chaste, plain woollen cloths were also available. When photographs are examined, the backdrops sometimes look a trifle battered or creased (*see figure 2*). Some had decades of use, and years of being wound on and off a roller took their toll. Sometimes, too, backgrounds can appear blurred or indistinct. This may sometimes have to do with problems of depth of focus, but often background painting seems to have been more impressionistic than precise, with the aim of suggesting a context without distracting attention from the subject. Backdrops are often to be seen in conjunction with incongruous props, so that woodland clearings seem to be curtained or furnished like a drawing room. There can also be problems of visual continuity, with the rustic illusion broken by a glimpse of the side or top edge of the backcloth (*see figure 3*), or with a sudden uneasy change of materials or perspective (*see figure 2*) where the background meets the floor and foliage encounters carpet or

Figure 2. Carte de visite; photographer unknown.

Figure 3. Carte de visite; photographer unknown.

tiling veers off at a new angle. In the studio of John Kay of Stranraer, open-air backcloth and indoor floor were firmly kept apart by a skirting board at the bottom of the wall.

Whilst it is appropriate to think of the professional portrait studio as aiming at a degree of sumptuousness, it must also be remembered that it was something of a chemical laboratory. The more successful studios might set up the processing and finishing operations in a back garden, and in the seventies and eighties the biggest concerns were able to employ numbers of (generally) women for printing, washing, gold-toning, fixing, hand-colouring, trimming, mounting and filing. In the smaller business, however, a handful of people undertook the work, and all stages of the proceedings were carried out in close proximity to each other. A wide range of chemicals could be used in the preparation and processing of plates: wet-plate photography needed silver nitrate, collodion, iodine, pyrogallic acid and gold chloride, whilst daguerrotypes involved the use of chlorine, bromine, iodine, mercury and potassium cyanide. The chemicals could cause problems. They might freeze in winter; they could be inconsistent in performance, with the particular difficulty of persuading any two batches of collodion to act exactly alike; they could be euphemistically described as odour-rich; they were, as will be seen later, dangerous. There was, furthermore, always an urgency about the whole process in the wet-plate era, for only while the coating stayed moist did it remain sensitive. Glass had to be prepared at the last moment, and pictures had to be taken and processing started before the collodion dried.

It is easy to overlook the strange impression that must have been made on our ancestors when they made their first visit to a photographer, were dazed by a display of opulence, and then led into the busy and strange-smelling atmosphere of a curiously (often blue-) lit room, wondering just what was to come next.

The Photographer

In considering the person who presided over this temple of photography, the first point to note is that he may have been she. In 1861 6.6% of workers in photography were women, and the figure rose to 26% by 1901 and nearly 30% in 1911. These figures can be misleading, for they cover all kinds of photographic employment, and only some of the workers were practitioners in their own right. In the large photographic concerns more women than men seem to have been employed in the processing stages. They were regarded as better suited to the exact but repetitive work involved, whilst the supervisory jobs were more often taken by men. But most photographers ran much smaller operations, and in these women often played a significant rôle. There may not have been many who started up a business alone, but an actively and often fully involved wife was not uncommon, and it was not only Mayhew's street photographer who valued women for their ability to relate to and direct sitters. Not unusual, either, was the woman whose increasing participation in the business led to her eventual taking over and working under her own name. Mrs Robinson, who was active in Ashton-under-Lyne in the 1880s, operated from an address previously held in the name of M. Robinson. Clearly her success and reputation were such, that it was thought useful to print 'late Robinson' on the back of cartes

when the business passed to T. Wright in the nineties. Ashton-under-Lyne was, incidentally, quite well served by women photographers, for Mrs E. Moss and Mrs J. Bardsley also operated there.

Since part of this book will be concerned with the statements made by photographs, it might be of some interest to consider here the kinds of statements photo-graphers made about themselves in the design of their card-mounts. It seems, after all, reasonable to believe that the image they projected of themselves played some part in influencing customer choice at a time when there was no shortage of photographers to choose from.

The idea of photographer as artist was a subject on which many felt deeply. There was much earnest discussion in Victorian times about photography as an art, and it is certain that many who took up the camera came to it from a background of portraiture. If, then, many used the language and visual imagery of painting on the back of their cartes and cabinet prints, it was an understandable reflection of their view of themselves, both natural as a way of thinking, and useful in giving some weight and status to their new art and their sitters. Thus, all possible variations of phrasing are used on the backs of photos: 'Art Photographer' (Reston of Stretford and Bailey of Pimlico) (*see figure 4*); 'Artistic Photographer' (T. Keig, Isle of Man); 'Art Photography' (Monsieur Sauvy, Manchester); 'Photographic Artist' (H. O'Shea, Limerick). Some exponents, such as W. F. Maltby of Islington, lay claim to both arts with 'Photographer and Miniature Painter'. Occasionally the message is conveyed with greater subtlety, as with R. Banks of Manchester, whose address is Rembrandt House. The image of photographer as artist is often reinforced pictorially. Most common is the appearance of palette and brushes, as used by David Brooks of Burnley and J. Jeanes of Pennsylvania, and sometimes a padded support stick is added

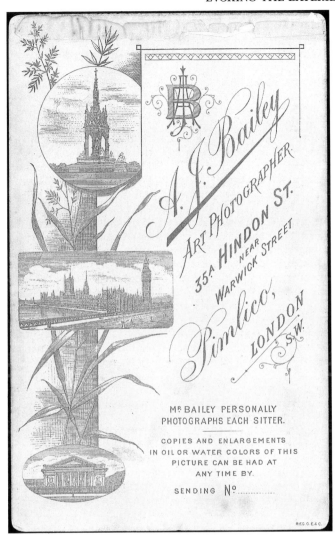

Figure 4. Cabinet print; A.J. Bailey, Pimlico, London

to these, as by Hampton of Glasgow. Easels figure prominently (F. Cole of Euston Road and F. W. Miller of Fakenham), but J. W. Thomas of Hastings goes one stage further, with a woman painting a portrait, and E. D. Spencer of Borough depicts two cherubs, one with a camera and one, looking rather bored, with a sketch pad. The female painter who appears on the

Thomas carte also appears on the cartes of W. M. Phillips of Southampton and R. Hammond of Bacup, indicating that designs could be selected from a range and were not necessarily individually designed.

In fact, the claim to artistic status was often not unreasonable. Certainly photography inherited much from art. Painters already approved of the even lighting of north-facing windows, and figures leaning on furniture or resting chins on hands were favoured by artists, who, after all, had to keep sitters still for even longer periods. Backcloths, too, owed something to art. In oil paintings subjects were sometimes placed in classical settings with a landscape background, thus suggesting social status and extensive property. In photographs the middle classes readily embraced the same kind of emblematic approach.

If artistic impressions mattered, so, too, did the idea of nature. Naturalness and truth to life are sought in portraits, and what is more natural than nature? The very images of photography were formed by natural light, and Fox Talbot had called the first photographically illustrated book *The Pencil of Nature*. Not surprisingly, therefore, birds, ferns, butterflies and flowers are often represented on cardmounts, sometimes mixed together with the symbols of art. Charles Mizon of Haverhill offers an image combining camera, palette and lily of the valley, whilst R. Banks, he of Rembrandt House, spells out his name in twigs.

As well as aiming to confer artistic dignity upon themselves, photographers sought to enhance their social status. Perhaps the best way of doing this was to be able to claim royal patronage. If such patronage was official, the wording 'By appointment to...' might be used, signifying that a royal warrant had been issued by the Lord Chamberlain. Those who had photographed royalty (or photographed at its command), but who had not actually been granted a warrant, tended to seek a form of wording which made the most of the connection, such as 'Photographer to...' or 'Under Royal Patronage'. Some printed 'By appointment' on their cards without authorisation, and there was much abuse of the system before it was, to a degree, tightened up in 1880. Examples of cartes and cabinet prints dropping the highest names are legion. A. & G. Taylor, an early

photographic chain with four studios in London, thirty-five in the provinces and six in the States, claim to be 'Photographers to Her Majesty the Queen' by Special Royal Warrant'. This sounds convincing enough, though it appears that the company used the royal arms for rather more years than they actually held their warrant. Edwin Faulkner of Woolwich asserts he is 'Under the Patronage of HRH Princess Louise Marchioness of Lorne' and John Hawke of Plymouth is reputedly 'Patronized by HRH the Duke of Edinburgh'. Some photographers are carefully vague: George Hopson of Bideford shows the Prince of Wales' feathers, but without comment; Emil Vieler of Huddersfield displays the royal arms but offers no word by way of support; R. Cade of Ipswich has an unexplained crown surmounting his trade plate; and the Southwell Brothers of Croydon describe themselves, ambiguously, as 'Photographers Royal'. It should be observed that, even when royal connections are genuine, the photographer has not necessarily taken pictures of, or even met, members of the royal family. The Queen employed at various times and in various places a good number of photographers, many of whom were commissioned to record royal buildings, lands and estate workers, or to supply the household with stereo pictures.

Those photographers unable to suggest nodding acquaintance with the queen and her immediate family had to make do the best they could. Foreign royalty was one possibility (Hellis of Regent Street, 'Photographers to His Highness Akbaloddowla, ex-King of Oude'), and home-bred nobility and gentry combined to form another. Currey of Bolton and Morecambe lists the Duke of Devonshire, the Earl of Derby, W. E. Gladstone and others of the nobility as customers. Smith and Sons of King's Lynn settle for 'Under distinguished patronage', and one suspects that, had the patronage been very distinguished, it would have been identified. A particularly thorough example is from W. Audas of Grimsby, who has a Golden Jubilee cabinet mount bearing an indifferent portrait of a rather young Victoria, taking care to attach no claims to it, and who prints underneath: 'By appointment to TRH The Duke & Duchess of Connaught, & HRH Prince Albert Victor, also patronized by the Earl Of Yarborough, the Earl of Ellesmere, Sir Robt Sheffield, Bart., Lady Yarborough, Lady Ellanor Heneage, Mr Heneage, M.P., &c'.

Another way of acquiring prestige was to give oneself some civic status, suggesting that one was the town photographer. Thus F. Beales of Boston uses a picture of the famous 'Stump', the London Portrait Company shows St Mary Le Strand, and A. J. Bailey of Pimlico features famous London scenes, including Parliament and Big Ben (*see figure 4*). Others, like Smith of King's Lynn and Hampton of Glasgow, incorporate the town's arms into their design.

A final, if more timid, method of trying to raise oneself in the eyes of potential customers was to turn one's initials into a monogram, and the cartes of, amongst many others, R. S. Freeman of Notting Hill, C. T. Y. Dickinson of Sheffield and John White of Ipswich are examples of this practice.

Lest references to design details favoured by particular photographers should lead us to think of these details as fixed, it should be remembered that any one studio was likely to work through a series of mount designs over a period of years, and to try more than one kind of suggestion of status. Over the last thirty years of the century Thomas Boxell of Scarborough had at least eleven different carte mounts and made use of all the kinds of image-building device so far considered, with artistic cherubs, local scenery, monogram, sprays of blossom, a swan in reeds and royal arms all being represented at one time or another.

It has been argued that photographers were men and women of some artistic and social pretensions. One other characteristic, sometimes used as a selling point, must be mentioned. They were scientists, needing some understanding of theory and the skill and patience to carry out chemical processes. This fact had two consequences, one visible and one probably not. The photographer who took great-grandfather's picture was often a stained man, marked by the ingredients of his processes. He was also sometimes a sickly man.

The dark room was a dangerous place, full of chemicals that could be injurious to health. Iodine irritated the skin, mercury vapour could affect the kidneys, and chlorine was to be used as a poison gas in the Great War. Potassium cyanide, sometimes used as a fixer instead of hypo, was particularly poisonous. Some photographers washed their hands in the solution to remove the dark stains made by silver salts, and one, who surprisingly survived, bit through a lump of cyanide to break it up. In November 1865 *The Photographic Journal* carried an article drawing attention to the dangers of cyanide. This was not an isolated piece: the photographic press periodically discussed the effect of chemicals on the health of photographers. Both *The British Journal of Photography* and *The Photographic News* kept the issue alive through the sixties and seventies, and in January 1887 the former publication claimed that Bright's disease, associated with cerebral disturbance in its advanced stages, was an occupational hazard of photographers. Examples of ill-health amongst exponents are not very hard to find. In 1860 Walter Messer retired from photography complaining of the effects of chemical fumes. and in 1864 his employer, Henry Peach Robinson, retired (temporarily as it turned out) at the age of thirty-four, his health damaged by the constant inhalation of collodion and other fumes. George Washington Wilson was forced into retirement by growing ill-health in 1888. Epilepsy was diagnosed, but his biographer speculates that he too was suffering from chemical poisoning and perhaps an addiction to ether fumes Wilson's decline appears to have been dramatic, unpleasant and unreversed. It is possible, therefore, that our family photos may have cost something more than the price paid for them by our ancestors.

Suggestions for Dress

When the attempts of such as Beard and Mayall to provide clothes for clients proved resistible, photographers generally contented themselves with offering advice on dress, sometimes in the form of a booklet issued to intending sitters. This was not, as it might at first appear, an attempt at sartorial tyranny with photographers setting themselves up to pronounce on fashion or propriety. Early photographic materials showed a degree of arbitrariness in their sensitivity to certain colours, over-responding to some whilst being relatively insensitive to others. The results, in monochrome, could be decidedly unsatisfactory. The choice of appropriately coloured or textured clothes could lead to more convincing images, and it was therefore entirely sensible of the photographer to try to persuade subjects to dress in a way likely to produce an acceptable end-product. Just how early pictures represented particular colours will be dealt with in the next chapter. For the present, the concern is with our ancestors' experience of being photographed. As the Victorian era drew to a close and photographic emulsions improved, there was less and less need to guide the sitter's choice of dress, though some problems persisted into the late 1880s. Certainly up to and including the sixties, direction in the matter of dress was desirable. Although after 1870 some colours were still best avoided, it is to the earlier years that surviving examples of advice generally belong.

Beard's studio, in the 1840s, recommended that black should be avoided, and that white frills should not be worn. Dr Andrew Wyatt, in *The People's Journal*, 1846, was more precise in his suggestions for daguerrotype sitters. He was for avoiding pure white as much as possible, and warned against colours in the mauve/violet range. He also held views on fabrics, believing that satin and shot silk gave a useful play of light and shade and pronouncing in favour of plaids, with their built-in texture and contrasts.

During the 1850s Mayall's studio was suggesting that women wear dresses of dark silks or satin, and listing shot silk and checked, striped or figured material as suitable, provided that it was not too pale. Again, there is the preference for material with pattern, texture or an ability to catch the light. Colours especially to be avoided were white, light blue and pink. Dark colours were generally fine, but black velvet was rejected for its great density. Men's waistcoats received attention, with black, check, plaid or fancy all thought better than white. For children, plaid, striped or figured dresses were the order of the day. In the same decade, in 1857, H P Robinson ruled that 'dark silks and satins are most suitable for ladies', whilst black velvet 'is somewhat objectionable'. White and light blue were proscribed.

In the 1860s a Norwich photographer enthused about silks, satins, velvets and lace as giving 'great richness of effect'. Cloths and merinos, he judged, gave 'quiet and sober effects'. In his booklet of advice to prospective clients, dating from about 1863, George Washington Wilson of Aberdeen assured ladies, 'The material is of little consequence; but it ought to be of a dark colour. Black, brown and green are the most suitable.' He warned against any extensive use of 'blue, pink, white, and lilac, or light purple', because the extreme pallor of their rendering made faces look dark by contrast. Nevertheless, problems with pale colours were clearly not as acute as they had been once, for, unlike Beard, he thought that 'a little white about the throat or wrists is an improvement', to prevent the picture from having 'a sombre look'. It ought though, he added ominously, to be 'as little as possible'.

It seems reasonable to wonder whether all this advice led to the clothes and material seen in photographs being uncharacteristic of the time. Enough clothes have survived to suggest that studio-wear reflected genuine tastes and practice. It was not that unusual colours or materials were being called for, but rather that certain usual colours and materials were left at home. Our photographed forebears were probably wearing perfectly typical clothes, but selecting from an existing wardrobe what was most suited to the task in hand.

Posing the Sitter

Victorian photographers, like photographers since, were likely to pay attention to posing the sitter to good effect. In his invented dialogue on photography (c1863) G. W. Wilson has a lady ask in what position she ought to stand. The photographer replies firmly that it is better to leave such matters to him, for the professional, 'if he has good taste and some knowledge of pictorial composition, ought to be able to arrange the position in a few minutes.' E. M. Estabrooke was alive to the danger of a tense and rigid patron staring at the camera with a face like 'a round white spot, with two holes for eyes, and a ... slit across it for a mouth.' Instead, he argued, the client should be at ease in handsome, comfortable and sympathetically lit surroundings, 'so that the result might have some claim to be called artistic.' Most photographers would have agreed with Estabrooke, but in reality examples of stiff, ill-at-ease subjects are hardly rare. Reasons for such unease will become apparent when the taking of photographs is looked at from the client's

point of view, but for the present concern is with the photographer's perspective, and Estabrooke was right about what could be, and often was, achieved:

'Photography takes the human form, sitting bolt upright, without an effort to soften or improve. Art comes in, and, behold! the pose is changed from rigidity to ease; the light is tempered and made to fall with softening effect upon the features; draperies are employed to give depth of shadow and brilliancy of effect, and the resulting portrait, instead of being barely tolerable – because of likeness to the original – is praised and valued highly.'

Just what percentage of Victorian (or any) portraits make the sort of transition from photography to art that Estabrooke described, may be open to question. But there is no doubt, from the evidence of surviving pictures, that a high proportion of photographers did give at least some thought to posing their sitters.

Some of the factors they needed to take into account were considered by Estabrooke. He was particularly unhappy about full-length standing male figures. Female standing figures presented less difficulty, since the lines of their clothes gave shape to the composition and gracefully flowing material disguised any appearance of stiffness in the stance. Men's clothes, however, gave less help, and for them the full-length standing pose 'should never be made without protest'. Objections to standing figures, of either sex, were even greater if the person was tall, and Estabrooke's solution was to go for three-quarter or half-length shots. It is interesting that this inclination to bring the camera closer, expressed in a work dated 1872, coincides with a general tendency in portraiture at that time to decrease the distance between lens and subject. In photographing 'short, fleshy persons', Estabrooke's advice was to move in closer still for 'bust pictures or vignettes'.

The shape of faces also received his

attention, with the general rule being offered that people with hollow cheeks or long faces should be taken in profile or semi-profile.

Compared to Estabrooke, Henry Peach Robinson sounds almost casual in his attitudes to posing, although we know that he could take great pains in setting up his pictures. In *The Photographic Studio and What to Do in It* (1885) he argued for keeping poses simple. To achieve a feeling of life and motion, he advocated having the subject walk around the studio and suddenly stop at the point where the picture was to be taken. He also warned photographers to make sure that the sitter's hands were in the same plane as the body, lest they should appear disproportionately large.

The practice of keeping hands in the same plane as the face seems to have been quite commonly adhered to. In the earlier days of photography this may have had as much to do with depth of field as with a sense of proportion. G. W. Wilson commented in 1855 that, even with a good lens, eyes, mouth and nostrils could be in focus while an ear was slightly blurred and the hair behind it distinctly so. He too, therefore, urged the photographer to organise the body in as much of one plane as possible. In practice, evidence of depth of focus problems in cartes and cabinet prints is rarely seen in such fine points as Wilson refers to, but it may sometimes be noticed that one hand, a little before or behind the rest of the body, is less clearly defined.

The organising of groups presented its own difficulties. Estabrooke felt that those of darkest complexion and dress should be placed nearest the light. In addition, he was quite prepared to make and act on judgements about people's appearance. Those who were good-looking should be set in the most conspicuous position, whereas 'the ill-favoured ones' ought to be placed less prominently, 'out of the line of sharpest focus'.

In touching on rules of composition, he voiced views that seem to have been widespread and, by and large, well founded. In arranging the figure and the accessories, perpendicular and horizontal lines were to be avoided. Lines should converge to a point or run in an oblique direction, with lines of support. He mentioned, as examples, a soldier resting on his rifle or sword, and a gentleman balancing himself with his walking stick. These precepts, as much those of painting as photography, were widely followed. Occasionally one can find examples which successfully flout the rules, as in a carte by W. and D. Downey of Newcastle, where an emphasis on the vertical gives the impression of unbending rectitude (*see figure 5*). More often, initiative in such matters is unrewarded. A carte by John Hawke of Plymouth shows two fashionable young women standing, three-quarter length, with arms linked. Each woman holds a rolled umbrella, with a hand at each end. One umbrella is held on the diagonal, though the angle directs the eye to an abdomen rather than a face. The other umbrella is held almost horizontally, cutting unhelpfully across the picture, and without quite matching the near-horizontal of the companion's boater. The linking of arms, crossing of umbrellas and two handed grips make for an unappealing visual tangle.

Directing sitters into assuming appropriate attitudes required some sensitivity. Estabrooke, as usual, had something to say on the subject. He stressed the fact that the photographer should avoid touching the sitter, admitting that many practitioners' hands were stained and damp. Taking the head of a lady between the palms, a practice he had observed, struck him as outrageous. The photographer should keep his distance, scanning the pose and issuing verbal instructions for adjustments.

If some photographers were capable of causing embarrassment or irritation to

Figure 5. Carte de visite; W. & D. Downey, Newcastle upon Tyne.

clients, the reverse was also true. Robinson was often made very aware of the vanity of his sitters. He did not care for those who wore new clothes specially bought for the occasion, and commented that 'the vainest creatures I ever have to deal with I have no hesitation in saying are the men.' Nervous sitters, too, were frequently encountered. Old ladies and old gentlemen were his favourites, because they were 'obliging and kindly', doing as they were requested and sitting where they were placed. One exception, though, to his observations on vanity and age, was an elderly marchioness, who insisted on trying to make her appearance younger and disguising her sunken cheeks by 'keeping a biscuit in her mouth while I exposed the plate.'

Clergymen as sitters deserve special mention. They tended to be respected and popular in their own worlds, and John Moffat of Edinburgh hit on the idea of taking ministers' portraits free, provided that he could sell copies to their congregations. But men of the cloth could be as alive to opportunity as men of the camera, and Robinson, when practising in Tunbridge Wells, was approached by a preacher with a similar idea. He demanded that a special backcloth be painted for him, showing bookshelves lined with evangelical works including, recognisably, his own, and he required a royalty on each print sold. Robinson acquiesced, considering, as Moffat had done, that sales to members of the flock would make the project worthwhile, but he ended up selling very few copies. It transpired that the preacher had visited several local photographers, making the same proposition to each, with the result that the town had a supply of cartes far in excess of demand.

The Ordeal

That sitter-tension should be a problem is hardly surprising. The Sunday-best clothes, chosen with regard to the photographer's instructions, will have made some feel rather splendid, but others self-conscious and uncomfortable. Opulent though the reception areas were, one of their purposes was to serve as a waiting room, and waiting rooms, however hard they try, are not generally relaxed places. Softened up by what, especially in the grander daguerreotype studios, might often have been a long wait, the customer was taken into the possibly strangely lit and curiously scented glass-room and posed. Not everybody enjoys being arranged, and any doubts about the enjoyability of the process may have been increased by the head clamp.

Head rests or head clamps predated photography and were originally used by portrait painters. Their purpose was to hold the head still during the exposure.

That they were not popular is indicated by a Norwich photographer's reference in the 1860s to 'the necessary but greatly detested and much abused head rest'. Their use was widespread in the early years of photography and continued, though with greatly decreasing frequency, until the end of the century. It is sometimes possible, in photographs dating from the sixties and seventies, to see where a curtain or table covering has been arranged over the base of the rest to conceal it from view (*see figure 6*). Drapery swept across at an angle rather than falling in a natural vertical line may be an indication of such contrivance. On occasion one can even see the base itself, its feet sticking out behind those of the subject (*see figure 7*). In the case of full-length sitting figures, it can be worth looking at the legs of the chair. Chair legs rarely, if ever, end in cross-pieces flat against the floor, and chair legs do not use to come in fives. There is more chance of spotting the base of a head clamp on male portraits, since nineteenth century women's skirts, generous in length and cut, are wonderful concealers of surreptitious items of furniture. From the seventies on, the preference for three-quarter length figures had the useful side-effect of cutting evidence of sitter-support out of the frame.

Figure 6. Carte de visite; Sawyer's Italian Studios, Norwich.

Once the subject was agreeably posed and less agreeably held in place, the photographer of the wet plate era still had much to do, while the client waited patiently. The image had to be viewed, lined up and sharpened on the camera's focusing screen. The lens was then covered and the focusing screen slid out and replaced with a dark slide or plate holder containing the very recently prepared wet collodion plate. The dark slide was opened, its cover being drawn aside, so that the plate was no longer protected against the light. Only then could the lens be uncovered and the light let in to create an image on the chemical-coated glass. This was the moment for which everything else

had been the preparation. Once the moment, or, more accurately, series of moments, was over, the lens was recovered and the dark slide closed again, to protect the plate from further light. Finally the dark slide was removed from the camera, or, in the case of multiple exposure cameras, moved to its next position.

Even later, in the much less complicated dry plate era, the sequence of events between posing the subject and exposing the plate caused a significant hiatus in proceedings. There was now no anxiety about keeping the plate moist, exposures were shorter, and more sophisticated mechanisms were available to regulate the passage of light through the lens, but there

W. H. Waterfield   DEVONPORT.

Figure 7. Carte de visite; W. H. Waterfield, Devonport.

exposures were necessary rather later than was the case, it is certainly true, even near the end of the century, that poses had to be held for what we would find an uncomfortable time. It is not possible to say what length of exposure was needed for any one photograph, but some general information may be offered. In the first professional daguerrotype studios sitters had to remain still for between 1½ and 3 minutes. As the process was improved, this time could be reduced, under good conditions, to between 3 and 40 seconds. In 1855, in the early days of the wet plate era, George Washington Wilson reckoned that an adequate exposure during spring, summer or autumn might take between 2 and 30 seconds, but in winter the time needed could be anything from 10 to 100 seconds. By about 1863 he was able to revise his estimates. His overall range of times was from one to 30 or 40 seconds, but his average exposure in the sunnier seasons was 4 seconds, with an average of 15 seconds in winter. During the sixties, about 5 seconds on a bright day and 15-20 on a dull one would seem to have been fairly general. H.P. Robinson considered 15 sitters in a morning a decent day's work, though in summer, using more of the day, he could increase the number to 20 or 25. In 1881, when he had made the change to the new dry plates, Robinson enthused about their sensitivity. Well-lit pictures could still take up to 5 seconds, but he was able to take indoor pictures in ordinary rooms, away from his well-windowed studio, in between 20 and 40 seconds.

The arrival of electric lighting in the eighties helped with further improvements of exposure times, but until then the photographer was very affected by the weather, time of year and time of day. During the working day the practitioner would have constantly to revise his estimates for exposures. G. W. Wilson observed that, as the light changed, new exposure times might be called for every

were still several fraught seconds while the photographer went about his business. As late as 1899 Frank Meadow Sutcliffe commented on 'the space of time which elapses between the removal of the focusing glass and the squeezing of the ball of the pneumatic shutter, while the focusing screen is bent or pushed aside and the dark slide put into its place, the tap of the shutter turned off and the front of the slide drawn.' During this period of time, he found, the sitter froze and needed to be brought to life again before the exposure could be made.

The length of the exposure itself added to the discomfort of the client. Whilst it is sometimes assumed that really long fifteen minutes. The weather was a very important factor. So much did it matter, that John Moffat, in the late 1850s, included an account of the weather in his week by week records of expenses and income. A week's weather and a week's takings were seen to be firmly related.

There were no light meters to guide exposure times. The photographer had to make his own judgement, uncover the lens, and then use a pocket watch, or simply count, until the time was up. Errors were hard to avoid, and some over- or under-exposure could be compensated for in the dark room. Wilson thought it better to risk leaving the lens open for too long, rather than for too short a time. As the sensitivity of plates improved, and before proper shutters were developed, photographers experimented with ways of achieving very short exposures by manual methods. One method was to hold a hat in front of the lens, instead of using a lens cap or cover, and whisk it away and back as quickly as possible. The resultant flourish, using a hat as prop, must have encouraged any tendency the sitter had to view the operator as magician, and suggests that some photographers may not have been averse to a touch of theatricality.

Even with improved exposure times, our Victorian ancestors had to remain still for a hundred or more times longer than is necessary today. With wet plates this period of immobility was much longer. Times varied, but they were the sort of times which might now, variously, be taken up by an athlete running a hundred metres, an average television advertisement, or even, in the days of the daguerrotype, a solo spot on 'Mastermind'. It is not then surprising that a certain stiffness is common in old pictures. Sometimes there is an odd appearance to the eyes: either they are unnaturally wide and staring, held open with such firmness of intent that they take on what has sometimes been mistaken as the look of a

thyroid condition; or there is a strangely filmed-over quality, which may be the result of a mid-exposure blink or two. A carte by F Walton of Leeds shows a family of five who, between them, exhibit both conditions: the mother has the other-worldly glazed look, while the son in the middle has the fixed stare of a B-film actor who has been taken over by aliens (see figure 8). One final point should be made about staring eyes. It is sometimes instructive to examine them closely, for it is not unknown for children of a later generation, given a book of photographs to look through on a rainy day, to amuse themselves with pencil or ball-point, filling in pupils with disturbing results.

An air of stiffness, discomfort and tension is an unsurprising feature of old photographs in view of the kind of experience the sitter underwent. Fortunately the side-effects of posing for the camera were rarely worse than that, but one occasion in 1844 deserves retelling. A photographer, working in John Plumbe's New York studio, realised that his subject had been achieving immobility by holding her breath, and that, after a heroic minute, she was about to faint. In a moment of panic, and seeking for something to revive her, he grabbed the nearest bowl of liquid to hand and dashed it in her face. The bowl contained hydrosulphate solution. The screech she gave was alarming, but clearly the liquid had its intended animating effect, for she at once attacked the photographer with some vigour. He fled, she followed, and a scene of some hysteria and violence was soon entertaining a grateful crowd in the street.

Perhaps more representative of the experience of most sitters, though, is an account from the diary of A. J. Munby for Saturday 22nd March 1862. Munby was anxious to build up a pictorial record of working women and often persuaded them to accompany him to the nearest studio to have a portrait made. On this even doubled fees was quite common. A head clamp could be used, and sometimes was, but until a child was old enough to understand its purpose, it was more likely to induce panic than stillness, and even Estabrooke, who believed that sittings should not be made without the use of the head rest, made an exception in the case of children. The best a photographer could hope for was to keep the required period of immobility as brief as possible. A Leamington photographer in 1881 recommended that children should wear light-coloured clothing and should be brought to the studio in the morning, when the light was at its strongest, in order to reduce exposure times. Not all operators were averse to children though. H. P. Robinson enjoyed photographing them and thought their naturalness worth the extra effort to capture.

It was reasonably argued that, if a child's attention could be suitably engaged during the vital moments, a sudden outburst of fidgeting was less likely. Eye-catching devices were thus brought out to capture their interest during the crucial seconds. Toys, bells and wire-balancing figures poised on top of the camera were all used, as well as the time-honoured birds. A carte by George Glanville of Tunbridge Wells (*see figure 9*) shows three small children, one a baby held by its sister, all looking to the photographer's left, their gaze clearly held by somebody enjoining their attention to some such device.

Toys could be very useful, since they could be held as well as watched, and studios were likely to have a selection for use when photographing children. It was also common to encourage children to bring their own favourite toys to relax them, for toys, especially dolls, can have something of a security blanket function. Large toys, like rocking horses, are obviously part of the glass-room resources. Otherwise though, without information supplementary to the picture itself, there is

Figure 8. Carte de visite; F. Walton's American Studio, Leeds, Boston & Southport.

occasion he took a 'dustwench' to be photographed. The preliminaries were gone through and the lens uncovered. 'They kept her several minutes, for the light was very bad; and wonderfully still she sat, not moving even her eyelids. But when it was all over, she drew a long breath and said, "Eh! Well, that is a punishment! That's wuss than a day's work, that is".'

Photographing Children

Any problems that adults experienced in keeping absolutely still were increased in the case of children. Early professionals were often, therefore, unenthusiastic about photographing them, and the charging of

GEO.GLANVILLE   TUNBRIDGE WELLS

Figure 9. Carte de visite; George Glanville, Tunbridge Wells.

WHITE   IPSWICH

Figure 10. Carte de visite; John White, Ipswich.

no sure way of telling whether a child in a photograph is holding its own or the studio's toy. Where the toy is obviously mechanical, its purpose is probably to intrigue, and this suggests it has been produced by the photographer for the occasion (*see figure 10*). The particularly loving clutching of a doll may, conversely, suggest a valued rather than a borrowed item. Generally though, there seems to be no way of distinguishing between sources of toys. There is certainly a strong tendency towards stereotyping in their choice, with dolls and, particularly low in play possibilities, baskets of flowers for girls, and drums, trumpets and whips for boys; but both parents and photographers would be likely to choose toys according to the same notions of what was fitting. Books, balls and hoops can readily be found held by children of either sex. Whilst in real life metal hoops were more likely to be used by boys and wooden ones by girls, it is unreasonable to expect to see this distinction reflected in portraits, unless the studio provided, perhaps improbably, a choice of hoops. Of the possible toys available, books and dolls had the added advantage that they could be quietly held, without the child feeling impelled to do anything with them. Seaside studios were likely to have a selection of buckets, spades and nets to go with a littoral backdrop, but, of course, children on holiday might perfectly well bring an item of their own beach equipment with them. As soon as it was possible, children could be treated and photographed as miniature adults, and they may be seen adopting grown-up poses and wearing more or less grown up clothes with a cool and confident air. A carte by John White shows a girl who can be no more than ten (*see figure 11*). Her hair is still worn down, and she is wearing an eighties' badge of childhood, a smock-yoked dress. But her pose is that of an adult. She is standing at a table on which there is an opened book. The left hand rests and the right elbow leans on the book, and her head rests on her right hand, with the forefinger pointing up the temple and the other fingers curled loosely down. The subject is a child, but the position is drawn from the standard repertoire for women.

Whilst the problems of presenting one end of childhood could be handled by pretending they were adults, the problems of presenting the other end were not so easily resolved. Babies needed their own kind of treatment. Many early photographers preferred, if at all possible, to take pictures of babies when they were asleep, for while they were sleeping they were as predictable as any other inanimate object. When they were awake, they had to be supported, for babies rolling off chairs made for spoilt plates and prickly parents. Studio machinery was clearly no answer in their case, so a human support was a common solution. Sometimes the babies are seen clasped in the arms of mother or sibling – sister at any age, brother if young. Older brothers and fathers are markedly less common as baby-holders, since cuddling tinies was not, in public at least, the sort of job for a chap. Alternatively, the human support could be hidden behind a cloth or fur-swathed chair, holding the

Figure 11. Carte de visite; John White, Ipswich.

infant through a layer of material, or, perhaps, with two disembodied hands protruding through and keeping baby in place. There are pictures though, where one suspects that luck has been trusted to and the baby has been put well back in a chair, packed round with furs, and the picture taken as quickly as possible.

By the end of the century some photographers had learnt that an infant need not be photographed in a chair, though most still settled for the planted baby effect. F. M. Sutcliffe, in 1899, wrote of focusing the camera on a part of the carpet pattern. He would then set the baby on the floor, letting it crawl, and taking the picture when it reached the pre-set point. He observed that 'no mother in her senses would ever put a young baby into a chair and leave it there.' The floor was both safer and more natural. It was partly improved exposure times that allowed Sutcliffe to adopt this method, but he also had a patience and an ability to contrive naturalness denied many photographers of his, and any, time.

Prices and Services

We cannot know exactly what an ancestor paid for a photograph unless, as in some cases, there is a price list on the back of the mount. Some idea, though, of the sort of costs involved may be gained from looking at a selection of prices.

Daguerrotypes were fairly expensive. Beard charged a guinea for a plain daguerrotype and two guineas for one that was hand-coloured. Two or more sitters brought a proportionate increase in price. When Watson and Fannin set up as Aberdeen's first portrait photographers in 1842, they too charged a guinea for a single plain daguerrotype, presented as a miniature in a case or frame. Two pictures of the same sitter could be had at the reduced price of £1.16s.6d. Larger prints cost two guineas, and the principals announced: 'Messrs Fannin and Watson think it necessary to observe that, from the superior and more expensive nature of their process, the above prices are so low that any future reduction is *utterly impossible.*'

The arrival of the wet plate brought a drop in costs, and when H. P. Robinson opened his Leamington studio in January 1857, he was able to offer ambrotypes at prices ranging from 4/- for a plain picture, 3¼"x2¾", framed, to 15/- for a hand-coloured and framed image, 6½"x4¾".

It was when the carte de visite was introduced, towards the end of the 1850s, that portraits became affordable by a large proportion of the population. When Robinson first offered cartes in 1859/60, he could charge a guinea for a sitting and twenty prints, but he had already achieved a degree of artistic recognition and was able to boast of royal patronage. Others charged, or seemed to charge, less. Robinson's cartes, after all, worked out at only about a shilling each, but many sitters would not require anything like twenty copies. More common practice was to charge for sitting and first print, and offer copies at so much a time. G. W. Wilson, in the sixties, was asking 5/- for the first carte, but a shilling or less, at different times, for copies. During the same period his local competitor, John Lamb, was producing cartes at about half his price. The difference in fees may, at least in part, be because Wilson had undertaken work for Queen Victoria. As a general guide, in the 1860s one might pay about a guinea for a dozen pictures from an up-market practitioner, but only about half a guinea for a set of prints by one of his less prestigious colleagues.

The seventies and eighties saw widespread reductions in prices, though again there is considerable variation. R. Wright of King's Lynn offered cartes at the rate of 'Six of any person for 2/-', and the London Photographic Company of Regent Street, advertising in 'The Times' in the seventies, provided twelve cartes for 2/8d and six for 1/8d. The Regent Street firm seems to have been unusually cheap, but not unique. Twelve cartes by Joseph Willey of Louth were priced at 4/6d in 1884, but for two photographic sessions with the same family in the following year he charged 2/6d a dozen. Where prices are learned from the backs of cartes, they are for copies rather than the original sitting, and these often seem to have started at a shilling, with reductions for larger numbers. Thus A. Henderson of London Bridge asked 5/- for twelve copies, and J. E. Bliss of Cambridge wanted 5/- for seven,

9/- for fourteen and 16/6d for twenty-six. For a very little more Bliss offered vignetted copies, starting again at one for a shilling and rising to 18/6 for twenty-six.

It was, of course, possible to have larger portraits, and, alongside his cartes in the middle sixties, Wilson offered whole plate prints, 8"x6", for half a guinea, with copies at 3/6d, and half plate prints at 7/6d, with copies at half a crown. When cabinet prints became popular, they made larger pictures very much cheaper, and in the 1880s Arthur James of Louth advertised a dozen of these for 7/6d.

Least expensive were tintypes. Those made by itinerant or back-street photographers were probably the cheapest of all, but even an established studio, such as Walton's of Leeds and Manchester, could sell them at three for 1/-, eight for 2/- or twelve for 2/6d. Tinting was one penny extra for each picture. Of the examples mentioned for cartes, only the cheap work of the London Photographic Company and the later productions of Willey could compete with such prices.

It might be noticed that simple portraits were only one of the things offered by many studios. In 1854 Wilson and Hay of Aberdeen also offered instruction and stocked chemicals, equipment and stereos on glass and paper. Robinson, in 1857, advertised a range of products and services: portraits and prints from brooch size to 20"x16", available, plain or coloured, on paper, glass or ivory; paintings and drawings copied and coloured; on-site photography of landscapes, buildings and estates; printing from amateurs' own negatives; mounts and frames in a variety of materials and sizes; local views and stereoscopic pictures; apparatus and chemicals; lessons given 'in every branch of the art'. In short, our ancestors may have come away with more than just portraits of themselves.

2. Appreciating the Artefact

In *A dialogue on Photography, or Hints for Intending Sitters* (c.1863), George Washington Wilson creates a conversation between a photographer and a prospective client. At one point the client confuses ambrotypes and paper prints and asks, 'Will you please oblige me by explaining the difference?' 'With pleasure,' replies the photographer, 'but the description will be rather long.' 'I am interested in the process,' she assures him, 'and will gladly learn.'

The reader may safely admire the measured politeness of this conversation without having to fear that a 'rather long' description of the processes is imminent. Something has been said of these matters in *Dating Old Photographs* and those who would 'gladly learn' are directed there. Some brief comments on aspects of three very common types of photograph will, admittedly, be offered towards the end of this chapter, but its main concern is with how the picture we handle relates to the picture our ancestor owned as new, and with how that relates to what the photographer actually saw. It is possible that obvious alterations have been made to a photograph, such as the exaggerating of pupils previously mentioned, or such as the rather more unusual case of the wife who was given to inking in hair on the photographed head of her balding husband. More importantly, though, the article may have been modified during processing or may have been altered with the passage of time. By their very nature, too, early photographs transform what the camera sees, for they are monochrome representations of a coloured reality. It is therefore to questions of what we, our forebears and the photographer see and saw that attention is now directed.

Deterioration

Flimsy and vulnerable though they are, photographs tend to last longer than the human beings they record. Nevertheless, time has its way with them, so that the picture we see is not quite the picture as it at first appeared.

Daguerrotypes, if their surface has been inadequately protected, may have become scratched, sometimes quite heavily, as it takes little to damage such a highly polished surface. The image has been formed on a piece of copper plate, thinly coated with silver. If the air has made contact with the surface, the daguerrotype may have become tarnished, in just the same way as domestic silver becomes tarnished. Green staining is also a possibility, if the silver layer has gaps through which air can work its effect on copper. Whatever the present state of a daguerrotype, we may be sure that its surface, silver or sometimes gold-toned in processing, was bright and mirror-like. Indeed, one can see one's face in a well preserved daguerrotype, and can, if so inclined, use it as a very effective heliograph.

An ambrotype may by now show, in the form of mould growth or water ring-marks, the signs of moisture invasion. Even more likely is a crazing or flaking away of the black backing. In its early state, however, it had a smooth finish, with strong contrasts, and the black was dense and even. The highlights of the picture are, and were, slightly greyish, but the distinct contrast with the black backing allowed this to go unnoticed and often, fortunately, still does, even though the backing has deteriorated.

Tintypes, or ferrotypes, often appear very dark with poor contrast and, in very many cases, they were no better at the beginning of their lives. But it was not uncommon to varnish rather than glaze them, and varnish is inclined to darken with age. It is therefore possible that examples of open-mounted tintypes, where a pinchbeck matt has been placed directly on the picture and folded over at the edges, may have been rather brighter once. Rust marks on card-mounted tintypes are, of course, caused by age rather than intent, and result from the fact that the basic material of a tintype is iron.

The vast majority of old family photographs are paper prints of one kind or another, and, whatever the type or process, they are liable to yellowing or fading. The same kind of deterioration, incidentally, is very likely to have occurred to any glass-plate negatives that have been handed down, and for the same reason. Poor fixing, of either negative or print, can lead to fading, especially around the edges of the image, for the common tendency of deterioration, whether mould growth or loss of image, is to work from the perimeter towards the centre. It is generally safe to assume that a yellow or faded image was of much better quality once, and that a picture faded at the edges was once an all-over picture. One must not, though, be fooled by the fashion, especially popular towards the end of the nineteenth century, for vignettes, where a central oval or round head-and-shoulders image is deliberately faded away into complete whiteness. The tentative thought occurs that, since, by the time the vignette became such a widespread taste, it was evident that photographs can fade, part of the format's attraction could have been its suggestion of artful antiquity.

Another blemish by no means rare on paper prints is the finger mark. While touching the image can have deleterious effects over the years, a bold fingerprint is likely to be the result of careless handling of negative or print during processing rather than of later injudicious treatment. A photographer in a hurry, with hands contaminated by chemicals appropriate to a different stage of the process, could sign his work with a clarity which would warm the heart of a forensic scientist.

Some kinds of deterioration have to do with specific types of printing. On platinum prints foxing, or brown spots, can appear on the image as a result of the rusting of specks of metal embedded in the surface. Foxing can also occur on other types of prints, as a result of their being mounted on poor quality, acidic card. Gelatine prints often have, especially in the dark areas of the picture, a grape-like bloom that was not originally there (*see figure 12*). Gelatine silver bromide printing was often used for early roll film pictures, so many snapshots show evidence of this phenomenon. What happens is that the gelatine absorbs moisture which in turn affects the silver content of the emulsion, resulting in a hazy silvering which is most apparent where it contrasts most strongly with the darker tones of the image.

For many years the most widely made kind of photograph was the albumen print, and, though many have survived, few have kept their original image colour. Highlights have almost always yellowed, sometimes to a considerable degree, and this may be accompanied by a fading of the brown tones. These two kinds of effect do not, however, invariably go hand in hand, and the colouring of highlights and the weakening of middle tones and shadows can occur quite independently. It is very likely, therefore, that the albumen print we hold today, often in the form of a carte de visite, was once a much more richly toned and more sharply contrasted article. The degree of fading, it might be added, is no sure guide to age, for sometimes older examples have fared better than more recent ones. In the period around the 1860s, the preparation of paper often included the use of more chloride than was employed in the eighties and nineties. This greater chloride content tended to

Figure 12. Roll film print; 'Freddie' album.

lead, via the attraction of more substantial silver deposits in the processing, to slightly better resistance to image-fading.

Gelatine was also used in the albumen print process, so these photographs, too, may have acquired a bloom that was not originally present. In moist or humid conditions gelatine is a nutrient for mould growth, and this can cause the prints to take on pink or purplish stains that no photographer ever intended.

One other way in which the picture we now see may have been altered, even if the print is relatively unaffected by chemical deterioration, is the album scar, to which cartes de visite and cabinet prints are especially subject. Otherwise mysterious marks on the surface may prove to match up with the edge of an aperture in a page of the album in which the photograph has been stored (*see figure 13*). Thus a cabinet print by Hampton of Glasgow shows a standing man whose dignity is somewhat impaired by a curved white scar which marries up with an oval aperture in the facing page. Over the years, pressure of the aperture edge has eroded the image with

which it has made contact. In a similar way, a carte of a young girl by W. Emmett of Stalybridge bears white marks forming an inner border, where the paper edges of its own aperture have pressed against top, bottom and sides of the image.

To sum up, the photograph we now handle was likely, when handed over to its sitter, to have been brighter, richer and more varied in tone. It was, after all, new. It wasn't intended as an antique; it just grew up to be one.

Flyleaves

The Victorians were alive to the fact that photographs needed protection, and one measure often taken in the case of cartes de visite and cabinet prints was a flap or flyleaf. A sheet of thin tissue, slightly longer than the mount, was stuck along its edge to the top edge of the back of the card. This flap was then folded forward, acting as a dust-cover to protect the image, whilst allowing a hazy impression of the picture beneath to filter through. Sometimes the name of the photographer was

Figure 13. Cabinet print; Frederick C. Palmer, Herne Bay.

printed on the tissue, perhaps with accompanying trade information.

It is not very common to find such a flyleaf intact. From time to time they are discovered, folded back behind a carte or cabinet print in an album. Extracting the picture from the aperture without damaging the flap is difficult, since there is usually no reason to know that it is present until the photograph has been part-way slid out. Then the tissue fails to follow cleanly, becoming crinkled or torn. Perhaps our forefathers could manage such an operation more skilfully, using some such device as Lund's photographic forceps, introduced around 1870. Clearly the Victorians were more often concerned with inserting than with removing pictures, but the ordering of photographs in family albums often suggests that some reshuffling has taken place. It is possible that this reshuffling has played its part in the loss of so many flyleaves.

It is usually simple to check whether a particular photograph used to have a flap, as a thin strip of adhesive, possibly with some tissue still stuck to it, is likely to be visible along the top edge of the reverse side of the mount (*see figure 4*).

Lost Colour

However much a photograph may have retained its youthful tones, there is still something lacking. Even if we see what the sitter saw on receiving the finished article, we do not see what the photographer saw in the studio, for the image is monochrome whereas the original was in colour. What is more, when translated into sepia and white, the colour values are often changed. If the same subject could be shot on both a collodion plate and a modern black and white film, we would notice significant differences in the way in which some colours were rendered.

Two particular problems attended early attempts to achieve a convincing monochrome representation of a coloured world. Firstly, there was the question of exposure time. It was hard to calculate how long to allow light through the lens when faced with sitters wearing extreme contrasts of black and white. What was needed to bring out the detail of one was wrong for the other: satisfactory results with black led to burning out the white, so that no detail could be picked out from the snowy sameness, and acceptable recording of white left black dense and featureless. It is for this reason that early sitters were so often enjoined to avoid wearing white.

The second difficulty had to do with the way in which colours registered on the sensitised plate. The chemicals responded more readily to some colours than to others. Early photographs are therefore very likely to suffer from colour bias, and some problems with some hues persisted for forty or more years. This gave another good reason for professional photographers to wish to influence the choice of clothes, and the advice they gave becomes understandable when it is known how colours behaved.

In early photographs green and red tend to seem very dark, looking more black than anything. Even yellow and orange can appear unnaturally dark. Pink and pale blue look white, and the pallor of blue is carried over into colour mixes of the violet and purple range.

The problem with green was to a great extent resolved in the 1880s, when emulsions were produced that would allow it to register as a middle tone. Red, however, went on appearing as black very late into the decade, and pale blue could still produce a washed-out effect. P. H. Emerson, who started working in the mid-eighties, was still able to complain that blue sky came out white and that 'the reds overrun the other colours and are too strongly rendered.' Whilst green was, by this time, less of a headache for the maker of portraits, its differences in shade could not yet be captured to the satisfaction of the landscape photographer, and Emerson was unhappy with attempts to render it truly.

As time went on the remaining difficulties were overcome and white ceased to cause problems. Black, when not sharply contrasted with white, could be handled effectively for most of the Victorian period, as long as the actual material had some ability to reflect light. Black velvet was a continuing cause of dissatisfaction.

When we examine a Victorian photograph and wonder just what the camera saw, it proves impossible to tell exactly what colours were being worn. It is possible, however, to draw some general conclusions. Up to and into the 1860s any evident contrasts of light and dark material are probably more extreme and dramatic in the finished image than they were in reality. We can recognise in pictures from the sixties and, to a degree, the seventies that any apparently black dress may equally well have been red or green, but not dark blue, which would have registered as a middle range. Similarly, we realise that a very pale dress may not have been white, but rather pale blue, pink or lilac, and that it is not likely to have been yellow. It may be, too, that some of the seemingly white neckwear of men was in reality coloured. We may add, from a knowledge of fashion and the introduction of improved dyes, that dresses of the seventies were generally likely to be rather brighter and more colourful than those of the sixties, even though such differences may not be reflected in a variety of tones in the finished print.

The registering of colour had its implications for skin tones as well as for clothes. In view of the properties of red, it may mean that an apparently dark complexion is really more ruddy than swarthy, and that spots and blemishes appear to be unnaturally eye-catching – a possibility that will be returned to when added colour is considered.

In imagining what the original colours of the scene might have been, it is natural to include the backcloth, assuming blue skies, green foliage, brown fences and honey-coloured stone. In fact, there was no need to use a coloured backdrop for monochrome photographs, and there was a positive advantage to be had from painting them in black, grey and white, or, perhaps, dark grey, medium grey and light grey. Since colour could have produced odd effects, showing scenery with milky skies and dark, undifferentiated foliage, there was something to be said for avoiding it. A reduced palette could create the required effects rather more successfully. This is not to say that colour was never used on backcloths, but, the tendency towards brown tones of the early printing processes apart, what we see when we look at background scenery is probably very often quite close to the way it really appeared.

Added Colour

Early photographers were sensitive to the fact that their pictures lacked colour, and ways were devised to reduce this disadvantage.

A percentage of albumen paper was, for a while, tinted in various colours, with pink being the most popular. Dyes were added to the albumen before the paper was coated, so that, in the eventual print, the paler areas showed the base colour. Paper of this kind first appeared on the market in 1863, and it enjoyed a degree of popularity for portraiture in the seventies and eighties. The dyes, however, proved very fugitive, especially since they were used in a very diluted form, and the colouring has, therefore, not normally survived. But, though the original tint has long since disappeared, there sometimes remains a dingy buff look, not unlike that of chamois. This fading to drabness happened quite quickly and was already evident by the 1890s, with the result that tinted paper fell out of favour. Cartes which now have a rather grubby fawn cast to the highlights may well have been tinted once.

More successful were attempts at hand colouring. The tinting or part-tinting of dageurrotypes, ambrotypes and even tintypes was not uncommon, and paper prints lent themselves well to the technique. Studios looked to promote colouring as one of their services, and this option is often advertised on the back of cartes or cabinet prints. It increased income, and in 1853 Hay and Wilson of Aberdeen were charging between 12/6d and one guinea extra, according to picture size, for this refinement. Some examples of casual or clumsy practice can be found, especially on stereo cards, which were produced for a mass market, but colourists were often very skilled and their work, where it has retained anything of its original quality, may well be very delicate and impressive.

The pigments used often proved impermanent, and by now, if a picture has had any amount of exposure to light, fading is likely, though faint traces of colour may sometimes suggest something of a picture's former attractiveness. A once-coloured print may now have a rather washed-out look, as a fairly common practice, where hand colouring was intended, was to make paler prints in order that they should take the tinting more effectively. If, however, a picture is pallid but bears no hint of colour, simple fading should be regarded as more likely. Surviving evidence of some colour does not necessarily mean that the whole picture was originally thus treated. Certainly, some photographs were so carefully and thoroughly over-painted that they came to look more like specimens of the miniaturist's art. But colouring could also be selective, with a delicate blush added to cheeks and lips, or with a touch of gold added to brooches, watch-chains and heads of canes. Such gilding has tended to last well.

There was one other way in which pigment might be added to a picture, though in this case the whole aim was for the modification not to be noticed.

Retouching could be undertaken to remove blemishes or wrinkles. This could be done by careful spotting out on the print, using pigment and a fine brush, but more satisfactory was to make any required adjustments to the negative, so that the work would become an integral rather than an added feature of the eventual print, and therefore unlikely to be recognised for what it was. Blemishes would appear on the negative as white spots, and wrinkles as fine white lines. If these white details were carefully filled in with soft lead pencil or brush and paint, they would not register when the print was made, for the light could no longer pass through them. It is easy to see, in this, the photographer pandering to the vanity of clients, but it should be recalled that, in early processing, the redness of a spot could register as black on the picture. H. P. Robinson was a reluctant retoucher, but even he pointed out that blemishes or freckles, 'not unpleasant to the eye or in nature', would be emphasised on a print, appearing unnaturally dark. He was therefore prepared to fill in white spots on a negative, not in order to flatter, but rather to combat the exaggerations of early colour recording. On looking at an old photograph now, one cannot expect to see evidence of cosmetic adjustments to the negative unless the retoucher has mis-handled the work.

Three Kinds of Popularity

I wish here to turn attention to three kinds of popular photograph. It must be admitted that these notes on them serve as a rather arbitrary sort of appendix to this chapter. But there are aspects of each which, considered, may add to our understanding of them as artefacts.

(a) *The Albumen Print*

For some forty years albumen prints from wet-plate negatives dominated photography, and they include the vast majority of cartes and cabinet prints up to the 1890s. It seems, therefore, reasonable to know something of the paper that bears so many of our ancestral images, and to recognise the enormous contribution of the chicken to the history of photography.

By 1870, twenty years after the introduction of albumen-coated photographic paper sensitised with salt and silver nitrate, Germany had become the largest supplier of the world's enormous demand. Even when British or American firms made their own product, it was usually German, sometimes French, paper that they imported for treating. Through the seventies and eighties the German share of the world market increased, and by 1890, when widespread changes in practice were imminent, it was estimated that American photographers used four times as much German as domestically produced albumen paper.

If Germany led the field, Dresden led Germany, for it was close to paper mills, could draw on a good supply of cheap eggs, and had low labour costs. The process was carried out mainly by women and much of it by hand. Illustrations of a Dresden factory in about 1890 show eggs being separated manually, egg whites being beaten to a foam in large, steam-driven churns, albumen being fermented in casks, paper being floated on the albumen solution, paper being passed through rolling presses and paper being sorted and packed. The industry was of some importance. Dresden alone had a number of factories, and just one of these, the Dresdener Albuminfabriken AG, produced in 1888 over eighteen and a half thousand reams of paper, each ream being 480 sheets, 46x56cm in size. Since a ream needed nine litres of albumen solution, provided by 27 dozen eggs, it is estimated that in that year alone this single factory used over six million eggs. The thought of all those spare yolks nags at the mind, making one wonder about the cholesterol levels of nineteenth century Germans.

It follows that there is a good chance that any pre-nineties portrait we have inherited is printed on German paper. The glossier the photograph, the more likely German origin becomes. There were two ways in which the gloss of the paper could be increased, the first of which was double coating. Paper could be floated in the bath of albumen solution for a second time, and this gave an improved shine. Manufacturers anywhere might use this method, but the second technique was characteristically German and involved the use of fermentation. Bacteria occurring naturally in the albumen were used to set off a fermentation process to produce a coating which gave a higher gloss and which took toning well. Paper made by producers elsewhere was often improved by the use of albumen which had been allowed to age, but it was the use of fermentation by German makers which led to a particularly valued and glossy paper that was widely used throughout the photographic world.

(b) *The Tintype*

The tintype was quick and cheap to produce. It could be handed over in a few minutes, was not as fragile as an ambrotype, and, unlike paper prints, did not have to be mounted. In-camera processing meant that tintype production was well suited to the travelling and outdoor photographer. As a result, the tintype in Britain came to be associated with cheap, even impromptu, studios and with outdoor occasions like fairs and seaside visits. Open-air or makeshift arrangements sometimes led to informal grouping and a more casual air than is customary in old photos. Tintypes can also show us our ancestors in holiday mood and wear in a way that is otherwise rare before the arrival of roll film and the snapshot camera. But the fact remains that the tintype has for us a very down-market image. If it was made in a studio, it is likely to have beeen a studio of limited

pretensions, and its cheapness meant that it found some favour in those classes of society which the camera's lens had not yet consistently reached. This humble status of the tintype was reflected elsewhere in Europe. A German *Photographers* Almanac' looked on it as the lowest level of the science, and scathingly compared its practitioners with 'travelling gymnasts, jugglers, acrobats and menageries at village fairs'. If we possess a tintype, we might incline, therefore, to interpret it as a sign of the lowliness of the sitter, and we might well be justified in that interpretation, always provided that the picture is European.

It is very common for an old family album to include pictures sent home by relatives who have emigrated. Such relatives often made their new life in the United States and sometimes the pictures they sent back include tintypes. These should not be viewed in the same way as European examples, for a North American tintype may not be assumed to show an immigrant getting by as well as possible and still waiting to fall on soft times. In the States, where they originated, tintypes enjoyed a respectability that they failed to find on the other side of the ocean. Tintype albums could be found in many American homes and they were a standard feature on the menu of perfectly well established studios. Indeed, E. M. Estabrooke, the American whose views on the glass-room and posing have been quoted, was a tintype photographer.

The very names by which this kind of picture was known give an indication of its relative status. In the States it was referred to as the ferrotype, for it was a picture on a base not of tin but of iron. The cisatlantic term 'tintype' seems to imply a degree of worthlessness, as for us the word 'tin' came, irrespective of the value of the metal itself, to have connotations of the cheap, disposable and, possibly, nasty, which in later years were to be inherited by 'plastic'.

(c) *Vignettes*

The vignette, an oval head-and-shoulders picture fading at its edges to whiteness, became immensely popular in the 1890s. The vignette had, in fact, already been around for some years. H. P. Robinson was experimenting with the format for a year or two before 1859, when he introduced it as a novelty into his studio's range, displaying examples in his shop window. Also moderately popular for some time before the century's last decade were oval or round portraits with clearly defined edges. But in the last ten years of the century the true, graduated vignette came amazingly into its own, and family collections of that period are often dominated by examples of heads, plus a very little body, fading into and floating on an expanse of snowy whiteness. Their advantage is that they can give a clear and, by that date, quite natural close-up of the sitter. But there is something depressing about an album containing vignette after vignette. We get a good look at hairstyles and collars and, since the popularity of the format coincided with some very elaborate blouses, we can enjoy views of plenty of intricate frills and lace. We are, however, denied the rest of the body and the clothing that it inhabited; we miss the painted backgrounds and the lavish studio furniture and props. People seem to exist in part and in a vacuum. It is to offset these unexciting qualities of vignettes that some account of their making is offered. This may at least give to the artefacts a context that their subjects lack.

The earliest vignettes were made by taking a piece of glass of the same size as the intended plate and holding it over a candle, thereby blackening an area in the centre. Then, when the plate had been exposed and taken to the dark room, the smoked sheet of glass was placed over it, with the darkened area covering the space in which the sitter's head would eventually appear. The plate was then exposed again to the light, which passed through the plain parts of the covering glass, whilst the smoked portion protected the vital part of the image. The developed result was a normal head-and-shoulders negative surrounded by a doubly exposed black area. Printing gave a positive picture against white. The technique of candle-smoking gave naturally imprecise edges to the vignette.

By the seventies a patented process had been introduced, and this allowed the second exposure to be made in the camera. Glass slides with opaque centres were produced, and these could be inserted between lens and photographic plate. Thus, when the picture had been taken, the lens was covered, the vignette slide slipped in, the lens uncovered again, and a further exposure made in order to saturate the unmasked outer area of the plate with light. We may reasonably assume the use of some such system of masking in the welter of vignetted cabinet prints and cartes which date from the nineties.

A revival of vignetting is sometimes found in the days of the roll film, as amateur photographers experimented with their own processing. Such examples may be less a continuation of a fashion into the twentieth century than a case of a young photographer aiming to recapture the look of pictures of the previous generation. Any home-processed family snapshots in vignette format have probably been created by improvised means, with the crucial operation carried out at the printing rather than the developing stage. When the printing paper, covered by the negative, was ready to be exposed to the light, a piece of card with an oval hole would be placed or held over it, with the effect of masking the outer area of the paper and leaving it white. The blurred edge of the vignette could be achieved by making a series of small cuts into the card around the hole, so that some light would filter through the resulting fringe and produce an ill-defined, under-exposed rim to the central image. Alternatively, the card mask could be hand-held over the negative and paper sandwich, and moved about very slightly during exposure, to break down the definition of the oval's edge. Thus the development of the vignette ended, as it had begun, in the kind of makeshift expedient for which photographers have ever had a talent.

3. Interpreting the Image – Portraits

Though Trollope described the fashion for 'the bringing out and giving of photographs, with the demand for counter photographs' as 'the most absurd practice of the day', his contemporaries exchanged pictures with matchless enthusiasm. For some, perhaps, the mere existence of likenesses was exciting enough, but for many, too, a portrait was a means of expressing and promoting a self-image. A nineteenth century French cartoon, made up of two drawings, shows individuals of very different kinds before the camera. The first man sits straight on a straight-backed chair, grim-faced and lantern-jawed, staring suspiciously at the photographer. His hands are on his knees, his elbows are tucked in, and the pose is made up of a rigid assortment of self-conscious right-angles. The drawing is entitled, *Pose de l'homme de la nature.* The second subject sits easily, legs not indecorously apart, with left hand on left thigh and elbow sticking confidently out. The right elbow rests on a cloth-covered table, with the hand drooping limply but elegantly at the wrist, forefinger pointing downward. The chin is held up, the head is thrown proudly back, and a confident, possibly aloof, stare is directed along the nose at the camera. The effect is expansive and lordly. The caption reads, *Pose de l'homme civilisé.*

As Victorians grew more accustomed to the camera, 'civilised' poses became increasingly frequent, and the results often give us an idea of the subject's view of self. Often, too, they speak of the photographer's view of the sitter as an individual or, more frequently, as a type. The photographer, however, was only speaking for his age and was able, in the unlikely event of his tastes being questioned, to fall back with some justification on the argument that he was giving the public what it wanted. Sitters fell in readily enough with the photographer's idea of how they should project themselves, though it is not unusual for tension and the problems of keeping still to diminish the intended effect.

In seeking to understand portraits, therefore, we are considering not simply what can be deduced about the people in them, but also what those people would like to be deduced. The image may not just be a representation of an ancestor; it may also be an expression of the values, attitudes, tastes and interests of the age.

Personality

When we consider how far a sense of individuality is conveyed in portraits, we find ourselves dealing quite as much with what we may not as with what we may deduce. There is a danger of reading character into what is actually photographic convention. It took a really good photographer to show insight into a personality. Indeed, even with today's fast films, the making of natural, perceptive portraits is not automatic, or even particularly easy. It is not therefore surprising if early photographs are not always overflowing with character, though capturing personality became less difficult with the shorter exposures of the 1880s, and later Victorian pictures often suggest more ease and less glumness than earlier examples.

Unease is, in fact, a common characteristic of the pictures made by wet plate and earlier methods, and examples of stiffness, gloom, grimness and simple blankness abound. It has become a commonplace that the Victorians were not necessarily as stern or saturnine as their portraits suggest, and that one should not make assumptions about a sitter's nature on the evidence of a joyless portrait. An anonymous carte from

38

the 1860s provides an apt example (*see figure 3*). A couple have been placed before a painted backdrop of steps, terrace and trees. She sits and he stands at her side, his arm round her, hand on shoulder in an amiable enough way. But little care has been taken in posing them. Not only is the point where backcloth and floor meet undisguised and unsoftened, but the side edge of the backcloth is clearly in view, together with an area of the wall behind it. The couple are uneasy: his expression is one of glassy ruefulness and hers betokens vacancy. Yet there is no reason to assume that mournfulness was their dominating characteristic.

A lack of cheery spontaneity in early photographs is, of course, easily explained. Enough has already been said of the ordeal of posing to justify a fair degree of sitter-tension. What is more, the very act of photography was potentially unnerving to those still relatively unaccustomed to it. There may be an instinctive folk memory suspicious of processes designed to duplicate a person's image. It is not necessary to conjure up specific ideas of wax dolls and pins in order to feel slightly vulnerable when faced with a camera. Even the language of photography, 'take', 'shoot' and 'capture', is threatening. This argument may ascribe to our ancestors primitive responses quite inappropriate to the nineteenth century; it is, however, not difficult to find people today who confess to a similar latent insecurity when being photographed.

Personality may be expressed in interests, and indications of these may occasionally be found in old photographs. In practice, such evidence is more often found in later, roll-film pictures, for by then there was a greater chance of people being shown actually doing what mattered to them; but studio portraits may sometimes include a tie, say, which points to some kind of attachment or involvement. Here, as ever, it is easy to be misled. A photograph of my grandfather, dating from about 1916, shows him wearing a yachting cap with a sailing club badge. Yachting was not then an obvious hobby for an elderly slater in the London area. What was a popular hobby, and not just with youngsters, was the sailing of model boats on the extensive ponds of London parks, and it was to a model sailing club that he belonged. A further problem is that items apparently suggesting personal interest may actually be part of the photographer's stock of props. Sometimes, though, studio provision and individual inclination could coincide. A carte by Joseph Willey, dated 1873, shows a young man holding a rolled-up sheet of music and leaning against a suspiciously insubstantial piano. The mock-piano was, evidently, a piece of studio furniture, but its use was significant, for the subject, Fred Furnish, was indeed an aspiring musician.

One particular taste often alluded to in portraits, whether accurately or for effect, is the love of books. Holding a book, and perhaps sitting in a supposed study in front of painted cases full of painted volumes, is a pose which suggests a degree of earnestness and refinement. But a book is also a good way of occupying a subject's hands and of projecting an air of respectability. One particular method of implying that the taste was genuine was to have the sitter keep a finger in the half-closed book, as if to mark the place for returning to after the photographer had finished his work. Similarly, on a carte by W. H. Waterfield of Devonport, dating from the early eighties, the older of two brothers holds a book open, with his finger on the line, keeping his place (*see figure 7*). Thus, we are invited to infer, the scholar has reluctantly torn himself from study and affably acceded to a request for a picture before resuming the pursuit of knowledge. One is reminded of Shakespeare's Richard III arranging to have himself discovered at his devotions in the company of two clergymen, and humbly submitting to the interruption on the grounds that his inclinations must obediently give way to the demands of others.

One particular kind of book that was often used in portraits was the photograph album. To show a sitter leafing through an album was a means of giving an apparently personal touch, presenting the subject as part of a family, linked to others by ties of blood and affection. When it becomes clear, though, that albums were often provided by studios, and when, for example, the same one may be seen in different photogaphs taken by Turnbull and Sons of Glasgow, the sense of naturalness and the power to convince are somewhat weakened.

If body language can tell us something about a person, then posture is worth attention. This too, however, may be misread, for it is necessary to recognise that deportment could have to do with fashions rather than personality. People, to a degree, stand and sit as their clothes dictate, and shapes, such as the female S-bend figure of the late 1890s, are those of the age rather than the individual. So the tipped forward stance of women in the late sixties and early seventies speaks of neither greyhound alertness nor inebriety, but is created by the voluminous bustle behind, and often accentuated by a hat tilted forward on the forehead.

One pose popular for women, that of elegant pensiveness, does reflect a mixture of the socially desirable and the photographically convenient. Quietness and stillness were thought attractive in a woman. Since nobody could be photographed without being quiet and still, Victorian womanhood constantly shows the qualities thought so charming in the sex. Signs of animation or vivacity are rare, and this reflects both contemporary taste and studio necessity. The standard pose for conveying cool and unruffled allure was the seated figure, with chin or cheek resting on a supportive hand. This created an air of gentle thoughtfulness, whilst making it easier for the sitter to keep her head still. Another possibility, which could be used separately or in conjunction with the first, was to have the woman focus her eyes on something other than the camera, creating a faraway look and suggesting preoccupations finer and more profound than simply staring at the lens.

Sometimes, and especially from the seventies on, a degree of alertness was allowed a woman by having her leaning forward a little. In part, this probably ties in with the leaning fashion look already mentioned. Nevertheless, the half-length poses, where a young woman leans forward, with one elbow or folded arms resting on the end of a chaise or on a padded support, often seem to suggest an openness and informality that go beyond the convention of fashion shape. Leaning forward is a friendly, confiding posture, and the diagonal slope of the body in such pictures, whilst stopping a long way short of eagerness or invitation, can turn the traditional pensive charm into something a little more approachable.

If we direct our attention to young men, one of the qualities occasionally allowed them, especially when two or more are together, is a suggestion of high spirits. Not until the roll-film era do we really enter the world of larks and high jinks, but there is sometimes an element of breeziness in studio portraits of young men. A cabinet print by T. Keig, taken in the nineties or perhaps late eighties, shows five young men, all wearing caps – those instant providers of a sporty air (*see figure 14*). They are posed one behind another at varying levels, with each of the higher four leaning forward on the shoulders of the youth in front. The effect is of a pile of subjects, a joky human tower. Keig's studio was on the Isle of Man, and it seems more than possible that the atmosphere of jovial waggery has something to do with the young men being on holiday.

Figure 14. Cabinet print; T. Keig, Douglas, Isle of Man.

Class

The class of a sitter may, to a degree, be inferred from the kind of photograph on which he or she appears. The earliest studio portraits were expensive and were made for those who could afford them. An ancestor who appears in a daguerrotype is likely to have enjoyed some worldly success and security. The same might probably be said of any ancestor appearing in a formal in door calotype study, but there are few calotypes of this kind, since the process was never widely favoured by portrait photographers. The makers of calotypes were generally experimenting amateurs rather than studio professionals. They recorded their own social circle, certainly, but also cast a wider social net, portraying estate workers, as did Henry Fox Talbot, or fishing communities, as did David Hill and Robert Adamson. The calotypist was more likely to photograph people who interested him, and subjects might therefore come from any area of society, whereas more daguerrotypists were concerned with the paying customer, and their sitters generally belonged to the moneyed classes. The ambrotype brought portraits within the means of a wider section of the public, though they were still pricey enough for their subjects to be from the moderately prosperous middle class. Cartes de visite and cabinet prints widened the social spectrum considerably, bringing the artisan into the studio, and the least well-off were catered for by the tintype. A tintype is not an automatic guarantee of humble status, since the better-off might use the services of a ferrotypist on holiday or at an open air event, simply because he was the kind of practitioner who was there. Nevertheless, a tintype, especially if a studio shot, is a broad indicator of relative lowliness.

Cartes and cabinet prints show us a very broad segment of society, and it is therefore difficult, and often impossible, to determine the status of the sitter. It may be argued, though, that the class (real or aspired to) of the sitter might be catered for or enhanced by visiting a classy studio. Certain names were in themselves a mark of distinction. Any ancestor who patronised J. E. Mayall, Adolphe Disderi or Camille Silvy was moving in the best circles. There was a certain solidity, if not glamour about the well established chains, such as Hellis and Son, with branches throughout the London area, and A. & G. Taylor, with studios throughout Britain and beyond. In the vast majority of cases, though, what we encounter are the products of relatively small concerns, with from one to a small handful of branches, and with a name that has not made history. Here some indication of the studio's class may be gained from the back of the mount: boasts of medals won and royal connections, the more precise the more convincing, may be allowed to carry some weight, and fashionable addresses or lists of highish prices may be significant. The image itself may also, in its view of the studio, give us some feeling for a firm's

status. Carelessly taken pictures, where sides or tops of backcloths can be seen, suggest an operation with no great reputation to be kept. Carelessness about the line where backdrop meets floor may, however, be less revealing, since this seems to have been a matter in which the Victorians were prepared to exercise a fairly willing suspension of disbelief. Furniture, too, may be informative. Some real solid items, ornately turned and plumply upholstered, are more impressive than purely painted surroundings. In considering all these details, it is probably fair to conclude that the better class of customer favoured the better class of studio. It should be remembered, though, that photographers' boasts and sitters' choice of establishment may speak as much of aspirations as of securely achieved and recognised status.

The appearance of the lower classes in photographs may be difficult to detect. From the earliest days of photography there was some interest in its documentary possibilities. In the work of Hill and Adamson and of Frank Sutcliffe, for example, we see some concern for showing working communities as, give or take an eye for composition, they naturally appeared. But there were plenty of others who, perhaps unconsciously, wanted their pictures of the lower orders to fit in with a view of what they should be like. To conform to Victorian values, working men and women needed to be seen as industrious, poor but honest, and content with their lot. Labour might be hard, but it could be seen in romantic terms, as long, at least, as it was somebody else's labour. P. H. Emerson wrote of the poor, hard lives of his peasants, but his pictures suggest an idyll of rural existence, rather than serve as a social document in tune with his written observations. When H. P. Robinson wanted to show peasant girls in his scenes of country life, he dressed up young women of his own class.

When photographers sought out the lower orders, they depicted them, whether objectively or through rose-tinted lenses, in a workaday way. But when those same folk sought out the photographer, they wished to be seen at their most presentable. They, too, had their aspirations, and these included, on special occasions like visits to a studio, looking as much like their betters as possible. A. J. Munby's preoccupation with the appearance of working women has already been mentioned. His practice of dragging them, in their labouring clothes, into the nearest studio, went much against their natural inclinations. Their understandable preference was to prepare themselves for the camera, and once they were thus prepared, their clothes were not particularly indicative of their status. 'Prints of girls in their best clothes,' Munby complained, 'appear undistinguishable in style and material from those of the middle and upper classes.' He was not the only person to comment on the sartorial aspirations of the relatively poor. Employers objected to fashion consciousness in their servants, since it implied thriftlessness and ideas above their station. Given a portrait of known date, it may be possible to identify humble social status by establishing that clothes, though fine-looking, are somewhat behind the fashion. Being up-to-date cost money. But living in the provinces or being of mature years can also be reasons for looking a shade behind the times. Quite reasonably, the lower classes wore their Sunday best to the photographer's studio, and we should probably be rather cautious in using clothing to ascribe social place to sitters, when their contemporaries had to admit to the difficulty of doing so. Munby saw red and careworn hands as badges of class and was, perhaps, obsessed by them. One might look to be able to pick out in photographs hands that have toiled, but it proves harder than anticipated. Since the colour red registered unnaturally strongly

on early plates, the hands of servants and manual workers might be expected to appear rather dark, but this is not necessarily the case. In sketches of his beloved Hannah, Munby conscientiously shaded the hands in heavily, but photographs of her reveal no such darkness.

Whilst working people adopted the fashions of their 'betters' and tried to dress like toffs, some social mobility of clothing in the opposite direction was also possible. Certain badges of lowliness came to be more widely worn and, thus, no sure indication of status. The working man's cap, which had been around since the 1860s, became popular from the 1880s onward, in a new classless incarnation as the peaked sports cap, with adults and children of both sexes. The white overalls worn by servants for lighter chores had their equivalent in a similar garment worn by children, though the heavier, sacking aprons, worn for dirtier household work, made no such social transition. Thus a child apparently dressed as a housemaid (*see figure 15*) need be an example neither of juvenile domestic labour nor of the rich playing at being poor.

All this discussion of working people should not obscure the fact that the majority of sitters for Victorian professional photographers were of the middle and artisan classes, all busy projecting a Sunday-best image and a sense of respectability that will shortly be considered more fully.

First, though, it is worth noticing that class may be looked for not just in pictures of our ancestors, but in the pictures that our ancestors took. The subject will be returned to when seaside photographs are discussed, but it may be said here that, as the century came to an end, an increasing number of people began to have more time and money for outings and holidays. Leisure opportunities had been one of the things which distinguished between

W. EMMETT.   VICTORIA GALLERY,
          STALY BRIDGE

Figure 15. Carte de visite; W. Emmett,
Stalybridge.

operate a more expensive camera than a Box Brownie. Before the Box Brownie days, of course, any photographs taken by ancestors suggest an element of social standing, for until then photography was the province of the better sort, who could afford the hobby, and who could afford to go to places where it could be interestingly practised.

Character

'Character' means different things at different times to different people. In the context of the property market 'of character' means old and possibly decaying. In common conversation 'a character' is someone whose manners and habits are considered eccentric and, if they do not affect us personally, lovable. To the Victorians 'character' denoted an amalgam of socially desirable virtues. It meant not just the general collection of traits and attitudes which make up a personality, but rather a set of essentially respectable qualities which society valued. The sense of social position which they wished to convey in their portraits was not unconnected with character, for character was likely to bring worldly success. It was a moral concept encompassing solidity, worthiness, solvency and an assurance which was grounded in virtue. Respectability was at its core.

Among the outward manifestations of respectability praised by, amongst others, Samuel Smiles, the author of *Self-Help*, were cleanliness and neatness, sobriety, a sense of self-reliance and responsibility, the reading of moralising and improving literature, and family activities like Sunday afternoon walks. The family was an essential part of the idea of respectability, and was so often the subject of photographs that it deserves separate treatment as a topic on its own. The concern with presenting a clean and neat front to the world is

classes, and they remained so, in a different way. At first the simple fact of making leisure visits was an indication of status. By the turn of the century this was less the case, but if class was no longer the basis for excluding people from leisure opportunities, it could still be reflected in the kinds of opportunities that were enjoyed. So we can see status reflected in the choice of places visited and the kinds of pictures taken. As the masses moved into the more accessible resorts, the élite roamed further afield; whilst everyman could enjoy the roll-film revolution, somebody who was Somebody could evident, from the photographic point of view, in the desire of all classes to be recorded in their best clothes. It is also seen in the white, scrubbed doorsteps so often in view in outdoor photographs. Doorways were the face the family showed to the outside world, and thresholds had a duty to neighbour on godliness. In the context of respectability and its encouragement of uplifting reading, backdrops of libraries and sitters with books are seen to have an important function in suggesting the right sort of image. Reading, of the right kind, not only indicated education; it also smacked of sober and wholesome habits.

Naturally enough, other studio settings, too, could help to reinforce the sense of a subject's respectability, and often those features already identified as suggesting grandeur could also, because solid and substantial, imply character. Real furniture helped. Good mahogany tables, heavy drapery and well-padded chairs had a weight and reality that painted detail lacked. Density, in effect, carried moral overtones. Backdrops could also add to the impression. Classical architecture, noble columns, imposing interiors, expansive vistas all carried connotations of authority, prosperity and respectability as well as status. The backgrounds were those provided by the photographer, and nobody seriously believed that the subject was ensconced in her own stately home or surveying his own country seat. But the implication remained that these were fitting settings for their subjects and environments in which they were not to be thought of as out of place.

Reference to particular examples can best illustrate some of the ways in which character could be projected.

That stiffness which often inhibits the expression of personality in early photographs could, on occasion, be put to good use. A carte by W. & D. Downey of Newcastle (*see figure 5*), previously mentioned under the heading *Posing the Sitter,* may usefully be returned to. An elderly gent sits amazingly rigidly. The chairback is upright and his back and neck (aided by a clamp, the feet of which can be seen behind the chair) are ramrod-straight. Neckwear makes no concession to ease and seems to prefigure the modern surgical collar. Even the stick in the man's hand is held so as to create a vertical. Only the bags under the eyes sag. Otherwise he is the embodiment of uprightness. It is interesting how words with physical connotations, like 'right', 'loose', 'bent' and 'light', have come to take on moral dimensions. In this case, certainly, visual straightness has a striking emblematic force. The studio, too, plays its part in the general creation of an aura of respectability, for the Downey partnership photographed royalty and was responsible for a famous 1867 picture of the Queen, than whom nobody could be more respectable, and her dog, Sharp.

In a world where men held sway, the sitting male often comes over as a figure of authority and substance. More common than the Downey pose is the man occupying a chair with curved back or arms, taking up the full area of the seat as if to show he has every right to be there. He is shown at his affable ease, sometimes holding a cane, which is as much a symbol of control as a walking aid, or sometimes holding an unidentifiable document, as if breaking off from pressing business to be photographed.

An interesting, and only partly successful, example of this expansive authority pose is found on a carte from the 1860s by J. Douglas of Glasgow (*see figure 16*). The subject, John Macfarlane D.D., leans back, but leans perhaps a little too far. He sits at an angle with feet

Figure 16.   Carte de visite; J. Douglas & Son, Glasgow (C. R. Stevenson collection).

on another with three fingers folded under and the forefinger, with which the pastor might point the way to his trembling flock, stabs over its edge and firmly downwards.   Perhaps he is indicating the probable destination of those unwise enough to carp at the less happy aspects of his portrait.

The present aim is not to cover every possible kind of pose suggesting respectability, but to invite thought about the ways in which character may be conveyed in photographs. As a further example, therefore, the problem of what to do with a younger man may be pondered on.

A carte from the late sixties or early seventies by James King of Gainsborough and Scarborough shows a youngish man, standing, in a full length shot. His left arm leans on a chair back, his right is at his side with fingers loosely curled. The chair quickly became, in photographic studios, an item used for leaning rather than sitting on. It was a useful steadying aid, helping the subject to remain still for the requisite length of time. Here it is leant on lightly, forearm on chairback and wrist and hand relaxed, without any serious detraction from the overall upright line of the body. A head rest is used to give further support, as the angle of the drapery reveals, for it has been pulled across to conceal the base of the stand. The combination of chair and head rest is sufficiently steadying to allow the introduction of a little lightness into the pose, and the young man has been invited to cross his left leg in front of his right, with left toe resting on the floor. The diagonal thus formed agreeably echoes the diagonal line of the forearm on the chair back. The weight is taken on the right foot and the stance looks secure and upright, but the positioning of hands and left foot adds a note of casualness to the image. The man looks suitably

planted firmly apart, so that the corner of the seat may be seen between his legs. His right arm is draped over the back of the chair and on to the table behind. The angle of leaning, the position on the seat and the sprawl of the arm are in danger of pushing the impression too far, and the result comes dangerously close to suggesting dissoluteness rather than magisterial ease. On balance the picture is saved from this unfortunate effect by a series of redeeming details: the good doctor benefits from the weight and gravity of wearing two coats; his mouth is set in an expression of unshakable grimness; the lower part of the offending arm falls on one book, and its hand rests serious, and the pose suggests male assurance, but pomposity has been avoided. The stance may be more contrived than natural, but it carries its contrivance fairly lightly and the result gives some weight to a young man without overburdening him. Poses of this kind were quite popular, and similar examples are not hard to find. Indeed, King appears to have been quite fond of it, for another example of the same period shows a different young man and a different chair, but the same studio and curtain and the same deployment of limbs. With a young man of decidedly fashionable appearance entering whole-heartedly into the relaxed aspect of the stance, the effect can become quite raffish, but, soberly done, such pictures can provide their own slightly youthful variation on the respectability theme.

Family

An album often proves to be the story of a family, starting with two individuals separately or as an engaged couple, including their parents, showing their own children growing up, and giving some space to less immediate relations. Amongst such relatives are often some who emigrated, whose pre-departure photos served as treasured memories, and whose later pictures, sent home from distant continents, were a valued link. The family meant much to our ancestors, both as a pattern of ties and as a concept central to a way of life. Inevitably, attitudes to family relationships and assumptions about rôles within the family find an expression in the pictures of the time. These attitudes and assumptions may be largely those of the photographer, for he sets up the pose and the finished result is to his design. But there is no reason to see the average professional photographer as existing independently of his age. He may have had his own artistic pretensions but, as far as social perceptions are concerned, his

mental furniture was likely to be much the same as that of anybody else. Photographers belonged to families too.

Even if consideration is limited to the tightest family unit, a couple and their children, there is plenty to occupy the student of old photographs. In an attempt to impose some shape upon this plenty, discussion of family has, like Gaul, been divided into three parts.

(a) *Husbands and wives*

In looking at portraits of couples we are likely to be struck by the image of the dominant male. The wife does not necessarily have to appear humble and downtrodden: she was an important figure in the household. But she was not the most important figure, and the relative status of man and woman can often be read from a photograph. The message is not likely to lie in degrees of handsomeness of finery. A glossy and impressive wife might be desirable in the eyes of some Victorian men, just as a glossy and impressive car might warm the hearts of some men today, and probably for much the same reasons. This is not to argue that there was a lack of affection between couples, nor is it to criticise the values of our forebears. History was, in its values and perceptions, different from today, and it is foolish to blame our ancestors for lacking our own claimed understanding and sensitivity. There simply was, without conscious malice or arrogance, a different way of looking at the marital relationship, and there is often evidence of this in pictures from the past.

The message is likely to come across in details of the pose. Direction of gaze is one thing to look for. It may be that he is looking straight at the camera while her eyes are slightly unfocused (*see figure 17*) or averted, or it may be that her attention is directed at him while he looks at the camera or at something other than her. Body angles, too, can be telling, with his

Figure 17. Carte de visite; R. Roberts Willson, Walworth Road, London.

occupy the only chair, but he has, as a result, the advantage of height. He is above her, she is on a lower level, and the physical/moral ambiguities in our language are again brought to mind. But when the positions are reversed, the relative importance of the partners is not. When the man has the chair, the subtext may be that superiors sit while lesser mortals stand. An effective way of putting somebody at a disadvantage is to keep him or her standing while you sit. He who stays low captures the high ground.

A photograph of a different but comparable situation may help to make the point. A post-card format picture, photographer unknown, dates from the period of the Great War, or just after. Two soldiers stand against an incongruously floral backdrop. Each is neatly turned out, straight backed, stern faced, the proud owner of a splendidly waxed moustache. But there is a distinction between them. Two stripes sit; one stripe stands. This convention is common in pictures of groups of soldiers: the officers and the senior NCOs have the chairs. It is simply a question of rank. The implication is similar when husband sits while wife stands.

Whilst both kinds of sitting/standing arrangement may be found in portraits of couples, the image of wife hovering in attendance on seated husband seems to be markedly more common. The popularity of this pose owed something to royal influence. The Queen enjoyed the rôle of attentive wife and was happy to be portrayed beside a sitting Prince Albert. In their case such an arrangement was pictorially convenient, for he was a good deal taller than she. In pictures where both stand, a step was sometimes used to bring her closer to his height, but when he sat and she stood the disparity was reduced in a very natural way. What suited the photographer suited Victoria's inclinations, and what suited the Queen had the habit of catching on amongst her subjects. Thus

body square on and hers inclined a little towards him, even if her eyes are turned in the direction of the photographer.

Most revealing, though, can be the seating arrangements. It is common to present one partner sitting and one standing. Either permutation is possible yet, surprisingly perhaps, the outcome in each case seems to be to underline the male's importance. If the woman is seated, and the man stands behind or to the side, often with a hand on her shoulder or the back of her chair, the effect may be protective, or proprietorial, or both. You feel that the frail little woman is looked over and guarded by her husband. He may be the perfect gentleman, declining to photographs with this arrangement may have been encouraged by royal example, and it certainly seems that the Queen was very conscious of the implications of the pose.

A carte from the 1870s by Gregson of Halifax and Bristol shows an older husband sitting expansively, angled towards the camera. His wife stands to his left, sideways on so that her body is towards him, though her face is turned to the photographer. Her hands, one placed on top of the other, rest rather tentatively on his upper arm. In a cabinet print by C. S. Scott, dating from some twenty years later, the body angles are less uncompromising (*see figure 18*). The man sits, hands on thighs, looking at the camera, but with his body angled very slightly towards his wife, whose body is also angled slightly towards his, though her gaze is directed to the left of the lens. Her hand, with fingers curled, rests lightly and awkwardly on his upper arm. In these two pictures we can see that physical contact does not automatically create a sense of warmth, and that gaze and body angles both contribute towards the impression. That the participants in these scenes rarely smile also contributes to the lack of warmth, but too much should not be read into apparent solemnity of mien, since holding an expression could be such a problem.

Eyes, bodies and hands all play a part again in a carte from the seventies by J. Kennerell of Wisbech. Although the lens captures the direct gaze of the seated man, his head is turned slightly away from his wife. His attitude cuts him off from her, but though her face is turned to the camera, her body is directed towards him, and she stands almost sideways on. Her hands rest on his left arm, but any affection in the gesture is not responded to, and the placing of her hands is again uncertain: they do not hold his arm but are clasped together. It is as if women may make timid gestures of affection, but may not become

Figure 18. Cabinet print; Charles Stuart Scott, Stratford East.

too demonstrative or too presumptuous. This same sense of inhibited affection is seen in the wife's gesture as captured on a picture from the 1890s by A. J. Bailey of Pimlico. There are details which suggest some closeness: he sits, with a hint of informality, on a wall rather than a chair; each body is slightly turned towards the other, though hers is turned more than his; both look at the camera in an equality of frankness. But there is still a feeling of restraint, for her hand, resting in the crook of his arm, avoids over-enthusiastic contact: the fingers are lightly curled in on themselves and do not hold on to him. A seemly tentativeness is again the order of the day. We must, of course, with all these

F.S.HARRISON   ·   WALLINGTON.

Figure 19. Carte de visite; F. S. Harrison, Wallington and Upper Norwood.

examples, be careful about our conclusions. We are not necessarily finding evidence of wives slightly afraid of husbands, or even of cool relationships; we may rather be learning about ways in which closeness between husband and wife could properly be expressed.

A carte by F. S. Harrison of Wallington is interestingly different (*see figure 19*). It dates from perhaps the first half of the eighties and depicts a husband, who looks noticeably older than his wife, sitting at a table writing. He is angled a little away from the camera and his eyes are directed at his task. The wife stands behind him, her far hand resting, apparently, on the back of his chair, and her nearer hand

placed lightly on his left shoulder. Her body is turned towards him, but her head is partly and her eyes wholly directed toward the photographer. Her pose seems solicitous. This feeling arises partly from his greater age. But it is not just this which makes her appear caring and protective. The fact that the man on this occasion is given, by his writing, a reason other than unconcern for turning away from her, and the fact that her hand on his shoulder is open and making full contact, unite to give a softness to the impact of this picture. Moreover, the fact that it is her eyes that meet the stare of the lens gives her an authority often denied to photographed wives. An understanding of the less conventional messages conveyed by bodies, hands and eyes in this picture serves to underline just how it is that the more usual husband/wife photographs make their statement.

(b) *Parents and children*

Though our ancestors' families were often large, the size of a brood is not too often reflected in indoor pictures. This may partly be because large numbers were not particularly manageable in the studio. It may also partly reflect, during the early days of the art, a reluctance to meet the increased costs that multiple sitters incurred. Full family photos do exist, but rather more frequently the parents appear with a selection of their offspring – with just the little ones, say, or with youngest and oldest. When shown with their children, Victorian parents are naturally cast in a rôle. He is the paterfamilias, the founder of the line, the figure of authority, and she is his lieutenant, a figure of some, if less, consequence. We may, therefore, reasonably expect some of the implications discerned in pictures of couples to be repeated in photographs of parents and children.

It has been argued that men tend not to react to being touched by their spouses and even seem unconscious of their presence. The same male characteristic may often be seen when men are portrayed as fathers. Both by eyes and by body language Victorian men seem able, in photographs, to suggest they are unaware of whom they have married and what they have sired. Thus, on a carte of the sixties by R. Wright of King's Lynn, a father sits square on to the camera and staring at it, showing no sign of realising the presence of his young son, who stands to his left, with one arm stretched out and resting, close-fisted and awkward, on his father's. Those ingredients which so often make up a statement in pictures of couples are seen again here, where two generations form the subject.

When shown with children, a woman often seems as unbending as a man, as if his authority is invested in her in his absence. Thus, on a carte produced by R. F. Bertolle of March in the 1890s, a mother sits while the daughter, no longer a child, stands slightly behind her (*see figure 20*). Both bodies are angled slightly towards each other, but the daughter's is turned further. There is no physical contact. Though both look at the camera, the daughter's stance, with one hand at her side and the other behind her back, seems slightly apologetic, and there is no doubt that she is the less important of the two. A carte by Monsieur H. J. M. Hamel of Doncaster aims to show a softer side to motherhood. It appears to date from the sixties or early seventies, and it shows a mother with two young children, the smaller on her lap, the other standing and leaning against her leg. The leaning and holding, together with the woman's attempted smile at the camera, are gestures towards a warm family mood, but these are counteracted by the expression of one child and the positioning of the other. The bigger child is old enough to be thoroughly distrustful of what is going on, and shows it. The younger, though on the

R. F. BERTOLLE.   MARCH.

Figure 20. Carte de visite; R. F. Bertolle, March.

lap, is being held in place rather than cradled or cuddled. Its hands have been caught by the mother, in order to prevent movement, but, as a result, it seems to have become an item to be displayed, rather than a baby being held affectionately.

As with the problems of keeping a young child still, it is clear that the tensions we may feel in family pictures must largely arise from the fraught business of posing. There is, doubtless, much in the assumptions we make about Victorian families, but naturally expressed affection was not technically, and perhaps not socially, a very suitable subject for a picture. It does not follow that stiltedness in a photograph has to reflect stiltedness in real life. What we see is probably evidence of a mixture of truths. Radiant and spontaneous warmth was difficult to contrive in the studio, but it is also true that some sternness was expected of fathers and that children were, to an extent, for displaying and parading.

A good example of the tensions we find is provided by a carte by F. Walton of Leeds, dating from the sixties or perhaps early seventies (*see figure 8*). This time a whole family is involved. The parents, as becomes their domestic rank, are seated. They are side by side in the same plane, his leg brushes her skirt and contiguous elbows jostle for the same space, with his coming out in front. But his hands rest on his thighs and hers are folded across her waist. They are close, but only in the sense that rush-hour commuters are close. Three sons are lined up behind them, with four of their six hands each assigned to a parental shoulder, resting open in one case, but generally with closed fingers, which seems a common way of keeping contact restrained. A family warmth is presumably intended, though the attempt is perhaps over-enthusiastic, as hands seem to be everywhere, and the centre son is particularly ill-served, being forced to drape forearms rather awkwardly on shoulders of different heights. As is almost inevitable with a picture of the time, the stares are glassy, though what could have been avoided was the military effect of having all five square on and looking stolidly at the same point.

Whilst unspoken social attitudes and technical difficulties conspire to make the characteristic Victorian family portrait stiff and uneasy, it is possible to find pictures which, on balance, give a warmer impression of relationships. A carte of about 1865, by J. Willey of Louth, shows a mother with three small children. The oldest child stands close to its mother, but looking ahead, and without any sense of contact. But the middle child, though

looking ahead, is sitting at the mother's feet and leaning against her legs, and the youngest is cradled on the lap. This cradling is, in itself, a little unusual, for the child is encircled by the mother's left arm, and not simply held up on display. What is more unusual is that the mother is actually looking at her child, and even looking with what might just be interpreted as an expression of affection. It is this unexpected but wholly natural direction of gaze which adds conviction to the picture. The success of the shot may partly derive from the fact that the family is the photographer's own, and may have been posed with extra care, or may simply have been more accustomed to the camera than many, and therefore more relaxed before it.

A carte by W. Brunton of East Dereham, showing a couple with a child, is in many particulars routine (*see figure 21*). The man sits; the woman stands. His face and body are directed towards the camera, which she looks at whilst keeping her body turned towards him. What makes a difference is the placing of the child between his father's legs and leaning on his knees. The easy familiarity of this position is enhanced by the fact that, if father's glance does not acknowledge his son, his limbs must, for the lower legs are splayed slightly outward in order to bring the knees in at the angle needed to give the child support. As a result, the photograph strikes an uncommon note of informality.

A final example of parent/child picture, a carte of about 1875 by C. J. Thompson of Norwich, shows once more that it is to details of pose that we must look for signs of affection, rather than expect the idiot beams with which later photographs abound. A father and daughter are shown in a rustic setting. A section of three-barred fence is set at forty-five degrees to the camera. On the nearer side the small girl is standing on the lowest bar. Her hands are in a muff, so she has to rely on

Figure 21. Carte de visite; W. Brunton, East Dereham.

her father, who is on the other side of the fence, to stop her from falling off. He stands close to the fence, leaning towards her, holding on to it with his right hand, and with his left arm stretched across and round his daughter, holding her up. Both heads are turned more or less in the direction of the photographer, but the angle of the father's body and the protective arm, which is performing a function rather than making a token gesture, are unusual and make a statement about parental concern instead of the more conventional one about parental authority.

(c) *Siblings*

In pictures of brothers and sisters we observe, naturally, some of the general features of the Victorian presentation of children. Children are often dressed as little adults, though the younger they are the greater is the tendency to treat them as dolls, dressing them up in sailor suits, or clothing them alike as a matched set. Identical or near identical clothes, incidentally, may also be seen as implying closeness of relationship. Older children tend to avoid the worst indignities, passing into young adulthood quickly once potential cuteness is over. Whilst the word 'teens' existed, the concept of a separate group was not really to develop until, after the Second World War, teenagers became a market. In Victorian times, teenagers were and looked like younger versions of their elders, though the tenderness of years of a young woman may be betrayed by the vestigial badges of childhood, hair worn down and short dress length.

When pictured together, children often show the coolness and awkwardness of their elders. A carte by James Bowman of Glasgow, probably dating from the late sixties, shows two brothers. The older leans with one elbow on a plinth, his right foot crossed in front of his left, in a pose aping adult assurance. His shorter brother stands to his left, left thumb in a pocket, right hand on the other's shoulder in a gesture intended, presumably, to be companionable, but more suggestive of making an arrest. Both stare glumly at something to the left of the photographer. Despite the hand on shoulder there is no warmth to the picture, and ease can hardly be expected, when he tangle of head-rest feet behind their own acts as a reminder of how the picture was achieved. In a carte from the nineties, photographer unknown, a young boy is seated, ill at ease, while his brother stands, leaning forward with right elbow on the back of the chair and left hand on hip. He affects a candid gaze and a man of the world air, and is very much playing the part of wise and assured big brother, though his junior seems in no way bolstered up by his presence.

Girls could appear just as uncomfortable and uneasy as boys. Two sisters, photographed by M. Huther of Londonderry, probably in the early seventies, sit side by side, but the younger is seated at a slightly lower level, to preserve a sense of rank. The older girl has her arm across with hand resting on her sister's far shoulder, but close enough to the neck for the gesture to suggest control rather than reassurance. The younger leans slightly inwards, with left elbow resting on her sister's right thigh, but though an impression of affection is doubtless intended, the fact that each stares ahead without quite meeting the camera's eye gives a sense of distance and coldness. Such failed attempts to convey affection are not rare. J. Willey of Louth had a penchant for having young siblings stand side by side holding hands, or with arms around each other, or, rather clumsily, a mixture of both, but the grim facial expressions tend to belie the message of familial devotion.

Nevertheless, what looks like genuine affection between siblings is by no means unknown. Whether it is real, or whether the photographer has been particularly successful in his contrivance, may be hard to tell. It may be that children would often respond more freely than adults to attempts to direct them. Such successful photographs tend to involve fairly young children, though it is not easy to determine just what degree of emotion could decently be shown by whom and at what age. A carte from the late seventies or early eighties, by Walter Luck of Tunbridge Wells, shows a boy holding a baby close to him, with heads touching. There is no sense of restraint. Though the boy is not tiny, he is still wearing a dress, and is presumably young enough to be seen cuddling a baby without loss of dignity.

Certainly a few years can make a difference to the kind of statement that is made. Photographed in the mid-eighties by W. H. Waterfield of Devonport, two brothers seem to have a gulf between them (see figure 7). The older sits; the younger stands, as if in attendance. The older has a book. Both look at the camera and neither gives a sense of being aware of the other's presence. They are not too close together – after all, they are chaps. Yet a photograph of the same boys, taken only a few years earlier in Ipswich by John White, tells a rather different story (see figure 10). The smaller one sits informally on the corner of a table, thus brought up to the level of his standing brother against whom he leans. Their bodies touch, and the impression is of closeness. But the passage of not very much time was to turn the older boy, for the purposes of photography at any rate, into a thing apart.

A series of pictures from the same family can reveal interesting transitions. Two cartes from the seventies show a little girl with her young brother. They were taken by John White of Ipswich, and the infant probably grew into the older boy of the last pair of photographs. In the earlier example he is still a baby, she holds his hand, and their cheeks touch (see figure 22). Both are a little older in the next picture, but they are still head to head, and her hand rests naturally on his arm.

It is dangerous to generalise, but there is a sense that it is acceptable for little girls to mother babies and small boys, and that boys still in dresses may be fairly demonstrative. Later, though, a cooling off seems to occur, until before they are so very old, children can suggest, through gaze, body language and seating arrangements, all those differences of status and rank that are seen in pictures of their elders.

Contrasts

The Victorians enjoyed contrasts in their pictures, setting tall against short, young against old, human against

Figure 22. Carte de visite; John White, Ipswich.

landscape and light against shade. The contrast between prosperity and poverty, though real and present, was less comfortable to contemplate and less likely to be depicted. This taste for contrast is, in studio photographs, most commonly expressed in pictures showing two generations together. Parent/child photographs fall naturally into this category. Sometimes three generations may be included, and sometimes the figures may be two generations apart. One of the most famous of generation contrast photos is Frank Sutcliffe's 1884 study, 'Morning and Evening', in which wrinkled and rugged Tom Storr cradles his infant great-nephew in his right arm,

while the child's small, pale feet rest in the old man's tanned and heavily veined left hand.

The contrast between generations may often be emphasised by a difference in fashion, though when we look at mixed age-group portraits, a clothing generation gap is often less striking than it would be today, for the young soon grew up to dress like adults. Nevertheless, one often receives the impression, especially with female members of the family, that fashion mattered more to the young.

An example of modest difference between generations can be seen in a cabinet print, dated 1904, by Frederick Palmer of Herne Bay (*see figure 13*). Elderly father and grown-up son are sitting side by side on the same seat. We see at once that the son has a higher collar and a pin in the knot of his tie. He is lightly moustached and has some hair, whereas his father is white bearded and balding. But each has a dark jacket with paler trousers, and each has a handkerchief in his breast pocket. The differences in dress are not, overall, particularly dramatic and though the picture is concerned with contrast, it also seems to suggest a sense of continuity. The two are linked by the same seat, but the father has put down his newspaper and taken off his spectacles, and it is the son who faces the camera more directly. It is as if the mantle of family authority is in the process of passing from one to the other.

An interesting variation on the contrast theme is seen in the carte by F. S. Harrison of Wallington, which was previously used as an example of husband/wife presentation (*see figure 19*). He is markedly older than she is, and the difference is echoed in their clothes. She wears the high bustle associated with the first half of the eighties, by which time her husband's frock coat would have been a trifle old-fashioned. She is still moving with the times, whereas he has reached the age at which one stays loyal to the sort of clothes one feels comfortable with.

Contrasts other than those of age find their way less frequently into family albums, but they do not go unrecorded. A cabinet print from the 1890s, taken by L. W. Thompson of Weymouth, relies on differences of height. An exceptionally tall seaman stands beside a lad who smiles up at him from around the level of the man's sternum. A strange cabinet print from the 1880s shows a white explorer, seated and dressed for the great outdoors, bare-headed, shirt-sleeved and with a scarf around his neck. At his shoulder stands a black warrior in tribal dress, complete with necklace, spear and elliptical shield. Behind them is the indeterminately befoliaged backcloth of J. C. Bradshaw's Manchester studio. Though the white man sits and the black man stands, both look directly at the camera. The contrasts of colour and culture are obvious, but the statement about social relationship, though apparent in the standing/sitting arrange-ment, is less marked than such statements often are in family pictures, and the warrior fares a shade better than the average wife.

Stereotypes

It will by now be evident that our ancestors tend, in photographs, to play the standard rôle alloted to them. Towards the end of the century an easing of the photographer's technical problems opens up the possibility of greater naturalness and informality, but social convention means that these possibilities are not always fully explored and that stereotypes outlive their practical need.

Most of the stereotypes have been mentioned already, and the aim here is to survey their range and offer a little new material for consideration.

Mature men tend, then, to play the part of paterfamilias. They are stern and authoritative, with a firm set to the mouth.

J. MᶜᴬᶜLEAN.   Nᵀᴴ WALSHAM.

Figure 23. Carte de visite; J. MacLean, North Walsham.

They lean back with assurance in their chairs or sometimes, unafraid of visual cliché, grasp their lapels (*see figure 23*). Mature women, too, have presence, though, if pictured with men, they tend to be overshadowed by them. As mothers they are, of course, devoted and loving, but these qualities are more often aimed at than captured, for the practice of instructing them to look at the camera instead of at their offspring, and the common need to act as a human support for a potentially wriggling infant, both tend to hinder the expression of maternal tenderness. Children are appealing, dressed up and displayed for the family album.

Older girls and young women are monuments to chaste loveliness. Often

Figure 24. Cabinet print; Shaw, Huddersfield.

encouraged to look pensive, they may also be required to carry flowers, age-old symbols of love and beauty, or ladylike accessories such as fans and parasols. White or palely virginal clothes are a distinct possibility once the camera has learned to cope with such colours. A cabinet print from the 1890s, by J. E. Shaw of Huddersfield, shows a girl seated, leaning against a heavily textured plinth (*see figure 24*). She is firmly associated with the beauties of nature, for the backdrop depicts foliage, there is a pot plant on the plinth, and she is holding a sprig of admittedly dead-looking leaves. The negligence of her grasp, the sinuous lines of the pose (with left elbow on plinth, body leaning to the left and head turned to the right), and the slight smile all

contribute to a feeling of cool, simple elegance. The hair worn down indicates her youth.

In contrast to the modestly and quietly charming young women are the dashing young, and sometimes not so young, men. We see the heavy swell of the sixties and later, with his exaggeratedly long Dundreary sidewhiskers. In the late seventies and early eighties the masher makes his appearance, with high shirt collar, fancy jacket facings and carefully barbered hair. Elsewhere we enjoy displays of incipient moustaches, waxed moustaches and burgeoning button-holes. A carte by Hall & Son of Brighton, which seems to date from the eighties, records a man with the hair of the masher, centrally parted, swept back and pomaded, but still sporting the Dundrearies of the swell, falling well below the level of his clavicle. He is no callow youth, but he still aims to make an impression.

Reading an Album

The fortunate family historian is confronted not just with a number of photographs, but with an album full of them. The album itself may be a splendid item, and a fair sum may have been spent on it. In the 1870s Parkins and Gotto of Oxford Street were advertising 5/- portrait albums in *The Times*, but during the same period Rodrigues of Picadilly was asking anything from 10/6d to £10 for interleaved carte albums with four portraits to the page and patent leather guards. The family album was a treasured home for a set of treasured possessions.

People represented in an album may go well beyond the immediate family and may include distant relatives, a selection of friends and perhaps even some servants, especially nannies. It should be remembered, too, that any couple has two families who, except through them, are wholly unrelated to each other. It can be fun to attempt to trace family likenesses, but two people who seem to resemble each other may actually be linked through marriage, friendship or employment rather than blood. Moreover, some of those pictured may have no connection with the main family at all. Cartes of the famous enjoyed brisk sales and might be included in a collection on grounds of admiration rather than kinship. The names of the famous were often printed on the mount, but not always, and the modern eye may not even recognise that a picture shows a celebrity of the day. This problem of recognition can extend to minor members of the royal family, though the main figures should be easily spotted, and huge numbers of portraits of these were purchased by ordinary folk. A carte of Victoria with the baby Princess Royal sold 300,000 copies. To complete the list of possible inclusions in an album, there are novelty pictures and pictures of pets, the family home and well-loved places. Novelty pictures featuring the obviously bizarre are readily identified for what they are, and such borderline bizarre images as those mentioned under 'Contrasts' may also come into this category. But there may be a temptation to try to fit into the family's circle mass-produced cartes of the picturesque working class or the quaintly British ethnic. Milkmaids and girls in traditional Welsh dress, for instance, should not be unquestioningly enrolled as relatives.

The ordering of pictures within an album may be an obstacle to sorting out who's who. Sometimes a chronological order may be evident, but often not. It is possible to find, several pages apart, pictures taken in the same studio and, from the evidence of a serial number pencilled on the back, taken on the same day. Where albums were designed to take a mixture of cartes and cabinet prints, any attempt at chronological insertion will have been foiled by the need to put pictures into apertures of appropriate size. Cabinet and

carte pages may be provided alternately, but few would choose the format of the next picture they took on the basis of the size of the next gap waiting to be filled. Often too, pictures have been moved around an album during its life. The Frederick Palmer photo of father and son, mentioned in the section on 'Contrasts' (*see figure 13*), bears pressure marks from what must have been a carte aperture in a facing page, but it now sits in an album opposite another cabinet print. Thematic grouping of pictures is not uncommon, with successive pages devoted to children, say, or to a particular branch of the family over a longish period. Occasionally there is evidence of aesthetic judgement in the ordering, with similar poses, full-length shots or vignettes perhaps, collected together, or with oval apertures used only for vignettes. Thus the order of photographs can play its part in hindering the reconstruction of a family.

One pleasure of an album, and, indeed, of old pictures generally, is the view given of a world different from our own. Here, too, we should be aware of the dangers of jumping to conclusions, and especially of making easy value judgements based on people's appearance. The hair of Victorians often looks lank and greasy. Sometimes, in the case of men, what we are seeing is a way of keeping it under control. Dry-look hair management may enjoy some favour today, but spray-on, quick-drying glues were not available to our forebears, whereas pomade and macassar-oil were. Greasy looking hair may, in fact, be hair that has enjoyed some attention. It is true, though, that standards of hygiene have changed. No doubt most Victorians washed their hair, and much else, less often than most of us. But then, what is easy for us was rather more of a performance for them. Another detail that could give an unfavourable impression of men is baggy trousers. The unpressed look does not have to indicate poverty or disreputability. The trouser press only appeared late in the Victorian era, and when we see smoothly pressed trousers in photos, they belong to the late nineteenth or early twentieth centuries (*see figure 12*). The Reverend Dr Macfarlane, mentioned in the section on 'Character', sports trousers of marked crinkliness, with signs of distinct wear at the knee, but it would be presumptuous to think of him as other than a pillar of repectability (*see figure 16*).

Clothes inevitably claim much of our attention as we study a family album. They are a very important aid to establishing the date of a picture. Conversely, if we have an idea of a picture's date, they can help us form a view of the sitter's sense of style and fashion, and it may be possible to follow an individual's changes of appearance over a period of years. In making judgements about adherence to fashion, we should remember that the provinces lagged behind the capital, that those riper in years might be less anxious to keep up with changes, and that, in the earliest days of photography at least, the clothing might belong to the studio rather than to the subject. The student of costume will be able to pick out finer points, recognising fold-marks on a skirt as a prestige symbol suggesting that a garment was new and fresh from its wrappings, or identifying a mannish jacket worn over the bustle in the late sixties as not so much up-to-the-minute as 'fast'.

However erudite the observations one may or may not be able to make, identification is usually the main preoccupation when dealing with a collection of family photos. One problem is that people's appearance changes with time, and that individuals who may look very different when seen as repre-sentatives of separate generations in the same picture, may look very similar at any one given age. Thus the young A may seem quite unlike the elderly accompanying B, but

surprisingly like a picture of B taken twenty years earlier. It is sometimes possible to take two people as one and the same, until an attempt to date the pictures shows that they were taken a decade or more apart, or that the carte in which the subject appears a little older is actually earlier than the one bearing the more youthful image. Caution is clearly advisable when deciding who is who, and identification should be corroborated by dating as far as possible. One minor observation might be made, which I have found of some use in deciding whether different images show two individuals or one. Ears, if visible, are very helpful, because they are little touched by change. Admittedly the prominent ears of the young may settle into easier cohabitation with the rest of the head as maturity is reached. But ears do not perceptibly gain or lose weight; they do not become hardened by adversity or dissipated by easy living. They neither pouch nor wrinkle. Attention with a magnifying glass to the ears may therefore prove a good way of confirming or disproving theoretical identification.

When the Smiling Starts

Major changes in the ways in which people appear in pictures date from the arrival of roll film and the snapshot camera. The 1890s saw the first mass-market cameras. Then, when the Box Brownie arrived at the beginning of the new century, photo-graphy became accessible to all. With this thoroughgoing democratisation of the activity came changes in the pictures themselves and a greater interest in the subjects being 'natural'. The shorter exposures needed for roll films provided the opportunity for exploring this interest, and the sudden proliferation of camera owners provided the means. Thus arose the beginnings of a demand for candid shots. Snaps could be made without pretensions. They provided a simple record of reality, which had a truth that the speed of the operation and a sense of complicity between photographer and subject encouraged. Professionals and serious amateurs were still concerned with composition, beauty and atmosphere, but alongside them were thousands who approached the taking of pictures in a more casual way. It was still necessary, with snapshot cameras, for the subject to stand still, for groups to be arranged and for thought to be given to the direction of light. But the process and the results were more informal, partly because of short exposures, and partly because on the other side of the camera was a familiar and probably uninhibiting presence. Pictures may have been set up, but they were set up almost on the spur of the moment, and the setting up was an undertaking in which the subject might feel a participant. Moreover, the very fact that snapshots had to be made out of doors took them into the world of play and relative casualness.

One very apparent result of the changes was that happiness entered the picture. Photography became a fun thing, used to record festive moments. The subjects were often in a jolly mood to start with. At the least, they felt inclined to go on record looking happy, and it was now possible to hold a smile for long enough to have a picture taken. Thus, though they are generally unpretentious and artless, snapshots seem to have, at their best, an appealing freshness. In fact, in their determinedly cheery way, they are quite as routine as the studio portraits which preceded them. If the Victorian photograph tends to make our ancestors look more gloomy than they really were, the Edwardian snapshot probably leans in precisely the opposite direction in the impression it gives us of real life.

An example of the new, relaxed mood is provided by a picture from a set of roll film negatives of which at least some depict Norfolk subjects. A family group has paused during a country walk for a photo to be taken. Clothes are, by Edwardian standards, fairly informal, two of the children seem to have their attention distracted by something on the ground in front of them, one girl is shading her eyes against the sun, and there are several smiles, though of modest dimensions. The man is central and seated on a wall, which raises him above the others. But he is leaning forward in an interested and unproprietorial way, so that the picture speaks of family rôles only as if by accident, and any statement is lightly made.

Another Edwardian collection, an album in which the only identified figure is a child called Freddie, includes a picture of the family taking tea under an awning in the garden (*see figure 12*). The garden awning and multistorey cakestand may seem to us a shade excessive, though perhaps no more so than some palatial patio furnishings of our own age. Mum's Sunday hat and Dad's boater would not have been considered unreasonable garden wear in their day, and it is rather an air of informality that comes over. The mother is smiling happily and holds her tea-cup in mid air. The cup-holding is doubtless posed, but it's the sort of instant pose that belongs to the snapshot era. Freddie has been caught, and very precisely caught, in mid-blink.

A third snap of the period, of unknown origin, also shows a group out for a walk (*see figure 25*). The man is off-centre. It is women who carry sticks, and on this occasion the symbols of authority are actually being used for walking purposes. The three women wear blouses and skirts, their coats having been rolled up and put on the ground. The woman on the left is ignoring the camera and appears to be inspecting the distant view, and she has one hand in her skirt pocket. The whole effect is pleasantly relaxed.

That shorter exposures contributed to the new mood of photographs is well demonstrated by another picture from the Freddie album. Here a baby Freddie, photographed in 1901, is held in one arm by his mother. A moment of open-mouthed spontaneity has been caught and his splayed fingers are recorded in mid-gesture. Though the image has deteriorated, it retains some clarity of detail, with the child's hand and the lace hem of his dress precisely shadowed on his mother's clothes.

It should be said in passing that, though professional photographers did not feel obliged to essay the relentless gaiety of the snapshot, studio pictures of the period often show signs of a new ease and naturalness. Mood is not, however, the only aspect to be looked at when the new photographic age is considered.

Roll film brought a different viewpoint to photographs. Most of the early popular cameras were held at waist level. This was rather lower than the tripod camera of the studio: though the professional photographer had to stoop to focus his camera, he did not have to kneel. The effect of the waist-level viewpoint was to draw the camera further away from the subject. Over the decades the studio photographer had moved gradually closer until the head and shoulders shot dominated. A close-up is not an easy or natural undertaking, however, for a camera pressed against the navel. The operator needed to step further back to fit the subject comfortably into the viewfinder or, in the case of the earliest cameras, to be sure of including the subject in the area pointed at without benefit of viewfinder. Because it is always easy to overestimate the space one person or object will take up in the finished picture, there was the tendency to step a little further back still. Indeed, box camera lenses could not focus on a subject that was too close. As a result, the full-length figure, which had become increasingly rare since the 1860s, suddenly reappeared, and the unnecessarily distant

Figure 25. Roll film print; origin unknown.

full-length figure was the subject of many pictures.

Another outcome of photography moving out of the studio is a new interest in the backgrounds. Non-domestic locations will be touched on in the next chapter. The present concern is with the background to routine family portraits, and that background was commonly the house or garden, for it was necessary to step outside to find enough light. Scenes outside the family home, especially by the front door, are common. Though the door may be open, lighting conditions rarely if ever permit us a look inside, but we can see the threshold, with the scrubbed step that was so important to the family's image of respectability, and perhaps the very popular potted jungle of shrubs and plants around the entrance (*see figure 26*). There may be awnings or blinds to protect the

Figure 26. Roll film print; 'Freddie' album.

paintwork or varnish of doors or windows, for this remained a common practice until well after the Second World War. The garden, like the exterior of the house, provided many a useful background, and, according to the pretensions of the family, we may detect beautiful flower beds, vegetable patches, flourishing shrubberies, clothes lines, trellises or pigeon lofts. There is always the chance of house or, less frequently, garden appearing as a subject in its own right, with human beings incidental or even absent.

It may sometimes be possible, from the look of the garden, to judge the time of year. Flowers are generally only broadly identifiable, and many, like roses, may bloom, as one variety or another, over a period of some months. But there may be signs to help us. One picture from the Freddie album shows the boy playing at sweeping leaves. His broom is full-sized, but he has a child's wheelbarrow. Fallen leaves suggest autumn, but there are not very many of them, the shrubs are still well covered, and some flowers are still out. It seems reasonable therefore to guess at that period of late summer or early autumn when the plants can't quite make up their minds to believe that the year is growing old.

Snapshot photography brought a con- siderable increase in the number of women photographers. Some women were active in professional studio photography in Victorian times, and room must be made in the Pantheon of early gentleman- photographers for at least two ladies, Julia Margaret Cameron and Clementina Lady Hawarden. But the arrival of roll film opened up photography to a huge female market. From the very beginning of the roll film age, Eastman was aware that women were important potential users of his product, and they dominated Kodak advertisements for many years, appearing routinely as practitioners rather than pin- ups, though sometimes, admittedly, as both. By the 1920s a Kodak trade circular reported that women formed the majority of snapshot camera owners and that they used them more constantly than men. They were also reported as being more interested in people than in views. It is difficult to identify specific results of this change in the pictures we see, but we may suspect that, if early professionals were right about their wives being skilled with sitters, women played a significant part in creating the easy and relaxed atmosphere that so often characterises the snapshot. We may certainly conclude that the majority of snapshot portraits that we now look back on were taken by women.

4. Interpreting the Image–Occasions and Events

Discussion of snapshots leads very naturally to consideration of pictures showing occasions and events, since, in the family album at least, such photographs coincide largely with the roll film era. In Victorian times studio pictures had been taken to commemorate happenings in the world outside, and this practice did not disappear in the Edwardian period. But more cameras were being taken out and about by more people and they were well suited to capturing significant moments where they actually occurred. The events and occasions to be considered may often be fairly minor, but they relate to life outside the studio, and the pictures deal with subjects other than the family, or with the family in a context. If portraits are often concerned with making statements, occasional pictures are often about proof. They are saying, in effect, 'We were here', 'We did that', 'We witnessed this', or 'This is evidence of a family milestone'. The snapshot picture has, in fact, never lost this important function.

Holidays

As the century turned, the seaside became (and long remained) second only to home and garden as the setting for pictures. Some professional photographers set up studios in popular resorts, especially along the front, and included seaside backdrops among their selection. Others simply went out and plied their trade on pier and promenade. But the amateurs were out in force too. Manufacturers, anxious to increase sales, pushed the idea of the camera as an indispensable piece of holiday luggage. By 1892 *The Amateur Photographer*, already well established as an eight year old magazine, was advertising its annual holiday guide with particulars of over

'Five Hundred Holiday Resorts and Photographic Haunts, forming the Best Guide as to Where to Go and What to Photograph.' By 1903 it was estimated that, on a bright day at the seaside, one person in ten carried a camera. It is easy to see why so many of the pictures we inherit are holiday photos.

In fact, 'holiday' often meant just a few hours by the sea. In the nineteenth and early twentieth centuries many of the visitors to popular resorts were day trippers. Very few working class people had holidays of any length, and even fewer had paid holidays. It was not until 1871 that the bank holiday was introduced, and this gave an enormous boost to coastal day tripping. On the very first national day off, in August of that year, the London railway stations were swamped by hordes of would-be travellers. Inevitably, when time was short, it was the resort most quickly reached by railway that received the trade, and those which offered a sandy beach were in especial demand. Rocky coastlines were much slower to become popular destinations, both because they tended to be inaccessible and because they lacked sand. Predictably, as working people began to pour into favoured seaside resorts, the more fashionable, who also had more time available, looked further afield. Thus a kind of class distinction entered the holiday picture.

Bank holidays did not start the social stratification of resorts; they merely accelerated an existing process, which had been helped along by the development of the railways. As early as the 1830s, in *The Tuggses at Ramsgate*, Dickens created a newly and unexpectedly rich family, anxious to embrace gentility ('Pa must leave off all his vulgar habits') and travel. Joseph Tuggs suggests Gravesend, but this idea is rejected, because Gravesend is 'low'. Mrs Tuggs' idea of Margate is 'worse and worse – nobody there but tradespeople'. They settle on Ramsgate.

It follows that the holiday location of our ancestors may echo their status or pretensions. The place chosen may be geographically obvious, since resorts had (and partly still have) their natural catchment areas. Thus the less elevated might be expected to travel the more predictable routes and patronise the closer resorts. But particular seaside places also had their own images and associations. The Isle of Wight, favoured by Prince Albert, had royal connotations, and the activity of sailing helped to keep it up-market. Bournemouth and Littlehampton were genteel. Brighton had outgrown its Prince Regent associations and was especially popular because easily reached by railway. The first London to Brighton excursion ran at Easter 1844. and at Easter 1862 132,000 day trippers visited the town. Its image might be described as robust. Leigh on Sea in Essex was popular with the inhabitants of East London; Blackpool found favour with the cotton workers, who could even walk there from the neighbouring mill towns; Rhyl was a favourite with people from the potteries. Where the masses went, funfairs, skating rinks, zoos and the like were created to cater for them and to consolidate cheerily down-market images. Sometimes neighbouring resorts shared the grades of society between them. Thus Yarmouth appealed to the working class, while the middle classes sought out Cromer and the coastal villages. Eastbourne was for those who wouldn't care to be seen in Worthing, and Hove was the acceptable face of Brighton. Occasionally a town succeeded in attracting visitors from a mixture of backgrounds, and Scarborough seems to have catered for quite a broad social range from Northern England. Cornwall and the West Country were far from the industrial centres, and retained their gentility until well after the Great War. Only the relatively well off could afford a week or two away, and such a journey could only be undertaken if there was ample time.

When we look at the pictures of our ancestors by the sea, we are struck by their dress. Full clothes for the beach are the order of the day in Edwardian and earlier photos, with no shortage of hats, ties, jackets, boots and high-necked blouses. A picture from the Norfolk set of roll film negatives shows three boys and a dog on the sand, with another child and three adults in the distance. Two of the boys wear sailor hats and there has been some removal of shoes and socks, but all three are dressed warmly, two wear jackets and one has a collar and tie. The adults strolling on the beach in the background might, as far as appearance goes, as well be walking along the High Street. The dog is blurred, because shaking itself dry, and seems to be having rather a better time than the humans.

One permissible sign of seaside informality in the 1890s and later was the rolling up of trouser bottoms. This custom must have its origin in the practice of paddling, but it may sometimes be seen in indoor photographs. Whether the trousers were kept thus while crossing the prom to the studio, or whether they were rolled up once there, in order to add a touch of verisimilitude, is not clear.

The tendency to remain well covered was not simply a matter of modesty. A sun tan was not seen as something to be sought until after the First World War. A result of this is that parasols, or umbrellas being versatile, quite often appear in seaside pictures, and children are often dressed in broad brimmed hats to protect them from the sun, though, the climate being what it is, they sometimes seem to be devoting much of their energy to keeping them on.

In spite of what has been said about the picture of the boys with the dog, holiday photos often have a jolly air, with the liberating effect of the beach encouraging jocular poses, improbable hats and, eventually, fewer clothes. Buckets, spades of alarmingly businesslike proportions, shrimp-nets and donkeys all make their appearance. Sandcastles are built, often by adults. The full *joie-de-vivre* of the beach is perhaps not seen until snaps of the twenties and thirties, when people stand on their heads, form human pyramids in the shallows, or bend over to peer at the lens through their legs. But even in the earliest snaps there can be a sense of hair being let down. In all this, the sea itself figures as a major attraction. By the end of the Victorian age bathing had really caught on. The sea had become something to swim or paddle in, rather than something to drink for health reasons. Paddling tended to be the social inferior of swimming, for it was an alternative that did not involve the cost of bathing machines or costumes. Those who ventured into the sea beyond knee-height had to dress both for the occasion and for decency. A picture from the Freddie album shows his mother ready for the plunge (*see figure 27*). She stands outside what appears to be a bathing hut (for huts and tents started to replace machines in Edwardian times). Her hair is done up in a turban and her bathing costume resembles a short-sleeved dress. Its dark colour, pale striped trim and anchors embroidered on the buttoned-up collar give it a suitably nautical air for one about to launch herself on the deep. A woman in the background is fully clothed, with high white blouse-collar, boater and ankle-length skirt. Each, in her way, presents a picture of smart seaside womanhood.

The countryside, too, could be a holiday location, and there was a well established Victorian tradition, amongst the travelling classes, of seeking out its more scenic parts and of scrambling up and being photographed on the lumpier bits. As with the coast, class distinctions became associated

Figure 27. Roll film print; 'Freddie' album.

with the countryside. Epping Forest was described in the 1890s as the 'Arcadia of the East End'. The Norfolk Broads at first enjoyed a high measure of exclusiveness, but in the last twenty years of the century they became increasingly the destination of the sailing and photographing middle classes, and the early years of the twentieth century saw a further broadening of their social range. Scotland was discovered enthusiastically in the wake of Queen Victoria, who first went there in 1842. The upper classes and well-off industrialists followed her example, and the bourgeoisie followed theirs. Not until the turn of the century did social change and statutory holidays begin to open up Scotland to the lower orders in even small numbers, and, like other remote areas, it remained relatively uninvaded by the bulk of society. An album of postcard format pictures, collected by Greta Carse in the

Figure 28. Postcard; 'Carse' album
(C. R. Stevenson collection).

early years of the twentieth century, includes a picture, dated 1912, showing a group of women sitting on the interesting rock formations of what looks like Staffa (*see figure 28*). One older woman, wearing a full-length coat, accompanies four younger women in ankle-length pale dresses. All have their heads covered, though two wear scarves rather than hats. But for the uncompromising ruggedness of the rocks they sit on, they could be in the park rather than in the Hebrides, and they add a wholesome and becoming demureness to the stony scene. Greta's Northumbrian family, with its teachers, its clerical links and, before long, its young officer, seems just the sort to find itself in the Scottish Islands in the early years of the reign of George V.

Mention might be made of the sending of postcards, some of which may have survived in a family collection. They may illustrate something of the sender's taste in holiday locations. But though postcards are now firmly associated with holidays, they enjoyed much wider use in Edwardian England, and their inclusion at this point has to do with our way of thinking about them rather than with that of our ancestors. In earlier days postcards might be sent to mark events, outings and anniversaries of any kind. They could be used to make arrangements or to announce visiting intentions, so quickly did they arrive, and they were often simply used for brief correspondence. They might indeed reflect something of their sender, but the taste shown may be for musical comedy in preference to music hall, rather than Eastbourne in preference to Worthing.

Family Occasions

Holidays are just one kind of family event. There were other kinds of outing, and the Victorians and Edwardians enjoyed their picnics and their Sunday afternoon strolls. In pictures of people out for a walk, though, there is often no way of distinguishing between full-blown holiday and half-day jaunt. Other moments of importance which we find recorded may include such subjects as the family's first car or an individual's first bicycle. But when family occasions are considered, it is the assembling of a clan to mark a milestone that first springs to mind. Often there is no visual evidence to indicate what a family gathering is about. The presence of a baby in long robes, say, may indicate a christening, but with many such pictures we know the nature of the event because of identification passed down, rather than because of significant details forming part of the image. As a general guideline we may say that, parents with children apart, the bigger the group the more likely a family milestone is being marked, but without additional help we may not know what it is.

Some family events, especially in the Victorian period, are dealt with in the studio rather than on the spot. The picture is to commemorate rather than actually record an occasion. Thus a child might go to the photographer dressed for a first Communion, or a couple might visit his establishment to mark their engagement or their honeymoon. The address of the photographer might give a clue to which stage of the relationship is being celebrated, according to whether the picture was taken in home town or at holiday location. If the wedding itself was preceded or followed by a trip to the studio, appropriate clothes and enormous, trailing bouquets may well be in evidence. It was not until the twentieth century that photographs at the church door became standard practice, so earlier marriage pictures had to be specially set up. Usually only a short time separated ceremony and image, but the most famous of all early wedding portraits were taken fourteen years after the event. In 1854 Roger Fenton was summoned to teach Prince Albert the basics of photography and to take his first royal pictures. Amongst his assignments that year was to take photos of the Queen and Prince dressed in their wedding gear. Victoria's dress still fitted, though it dated from 1840.

The kind of family occasion of which there is most evidence in old pictures is death. A common reference to death is found in pictures showing the wearing of jet jewellery, but jet was only part of standard mourning equipment. The custom of mourning predates the death of the Prince Consort in 1861, but practices became intensified and highly formalised thereafter, for in this, as in so much else, royal usage set a widely observed precedent. The stages of mourning for a close relative were distinct. In the first year

lots of black crêpe was worn, and may be looked for around the hems of skirts, in panels on the front of dresses, and covering sleeves from wrist to elbow. About nine months of half-mourning followed, with reduced quantities of crêpe. Then came three months when crêpe was dispensed with and plain black and white were worn. Once two years were up, colours could be worn again. In photographs, crêpe often looks dull and rough-textured against other materials.

If the date of a photograph is known, it may be possible to work out who is being mourned, but there are obstacles. Premature losses were not rare events, some people, like the Queen, continued in mourning for longer than the requisite period, and mourning might be undertaken for quite distant relatives and for friends.

Photographs were also used as ways of coming to terms with death. Memorial photos took more than one form. One practice, towards the end of the nineteenth century, was the placing of photos of the dead on their graves. Whilst the standard types of print could not be expected to weather the elements, portraits on porcelain could survive for a good number of years. Perhaps more common, and far more likely to be encountered today, are pictures in memorial mounts. These were sold to provide a fitting setting for portraits of the departed. In 1865 Maiben and Bingham of London advertised memorial mounts in eight different styles. Most suggested a framework of classical architecture, often incorporating such phrases as 'In Memoriam' and 'In Affectionate Remembrance of . . .'. Some had spaces for entering dates of birth and death. The pictures inserted in the mounts may have been favourite shots of the loved one when alive, but photographs taken of the dead were not unusual. In creating a visual record of the lost one, the Victorians sought to confer a kind of immortality.

SCARBOROUGH.

Figure 29. Cabinet print; Cromack, Scarborough.

This impulse was especially keenly felt by parents, and, with infant mortality high, it is understandable that they should attempt to preserve their last sight of a child.

Another kind of picture related to death is the tribute photograph. Portraits of Victoria in widow's weeds casting an adoring look at a bust of Albert must have encouraged this trend. Few families could run to a bust, but many could manage a tombstone, and so we come across pictures of graves, with or without attendant mourners. A cabinet print by Cromack of Scarborough shows the brother and sister of Tetty Mason, who died in 1880, aged 21. They stand on either side of her grave

(*see figure 29*). Each holds a single flower. The young sister, not yet in full-length skirt, looks with downcast eyes at the ground in which Tetty was laid. The brother, with flower-holding hand resting on the gravestone, stands with legs crossed in a pose that is oddly informal, though certainly not relaxed. His eyes are turned upward towards that heaven where he hopes Tetty now resides. The picture is probably not to our taste, and we may see the Victorians as having a mawkish attitude towards death. Perhaps, though, the truth is that we have become rather bad at responding to this necessary event, and are only now relearning ways of handling loss, rather than glibly trotting out such observations as 'Life must go on,' and 'He/she is being very good about it.'

Work and Play

Only a limited pictorial record of daily work has come down to us. Rural labour was photographed more often than factory and other town work, and the capturing of either was generally as a conscious contribution to social documentation, and therefore unlikely to find its way into the family album. With the popularisation of photography it became possible, though not especially common, for people to take pictures at their workplace, but in earlier days few workers of the humbler sort were photographed in their occupational gear in the studio, unless enveigled there by an enthusiast like Munby. Occasionally such labourers as fisher girls or female pithead workers were recorded for their picturesqueness, and the results, sold as novelties, might find their way into albums as holiday souvenirs or simply curiosities. It is a reasonable general assumption that, when workers chose to have their pictures taken, they dressed up for the occasion as everybody else did. Where, for instance, we find a picture of a servant dressed as a servant, we may conclude that it was taken at the employers' behest, for inclusion in their own album, just as they might include a picture of their dog.

Clergymen and soldiers are an exception to the rule that people do not usually appear of their own volition in portraits in working garb. In such cases the occupational dress carries its particular kind of status to which the wearer does not mind owning. Railway workers share something of this characteristic, too: the railway was a great symbol of Victorian progress and its uniforms could be worn with some pride.

Play fares rather better than work in old photographs. Sport, with its special clothes, was a natural subject for the camera, and sportswear had a sense of occasion that workwear lacked. Of necessity, early photographs, even those of the roll film era, more often show people ready for sport than show them actually doing it. Static team line-ups are common, with footballers and cricketers drawn up in arm-folded rows. Scope for action shots was limited, for even with snapshot cameras it was necessary to keep still briefly. The Norfolk roll film negatives include a shot of boys playing cricket (*see figure 30*). The batsman leans forward in a carefully posed stance, though his feet have not moved. The toe of the bat touches the ground, and is thus prevented from wavering. The boy at slip stands fairly casually, as if there is no real danger of a ball coming his way. The wicket-keeper contrives to look alert, as if he is actually reacting to events. The overall impression is of something happening, at least until one tries to work out exactly what it is.

As with holidays so with sport, associations of class enter into leisure activity, and one may gain an idea of the social milieu of ancestors from the activities they seem to enjoy. Cricket, tennis and rowing were all fine for the better sort of person, and a picture of Keswick Croquet Club in 1906 seems an appropriately middle-class subject to find in the album of Greta Carse.

Cycling, or, more accurately, people posed on bicycles, is a common subject and spans all sections of the community. It was a vigorous, healthy activity, yet respectable and practised by all classes. Also widely popular and possible throughout society was skating. Many of the earliest skating pictures predate the Box Brownie and come from the very cold winter of 1884-5. The freezing of the Thames was an obviously attractive event for photographers, but many less dramatic places were also used for skating. Londoners covered the lake in St James' Park, and others used ponds and dykes all over the

Figure 30. Modern print from roll film negative; 'Norfolk' negatives.

country. East Anglia was for many years a stronghold of ice activity, with skating and, in Edwardian times at least, ice-yachting popular sports on the frozen washes.

A sport with its own built-in class distinction is shooting. In pictures of men with guns, it is worth looking for evidence of what has been bagged. The gentry, fresh from an organised shoot, may display hare, deer and pheasant. Such quarries were 'game', and not for the lower orders, who, if they owned a gun and wanted something for the pot, were permitted to go after rabbit and woodpigeon. Inclusion of the kill in the picture may therefore help to socially place the hunter. Of course, it was not unknown for lesser mortals to shoot game, but, since this constituted poaching, evidence of success is not very likely to be presented on film.

Institutional Pictures

Between the worlds of work and sport there exists a wide range of other ways in which people organise themselves, and some of these may be reflected in old photos of members in a group or of individuals dressed to show their affiliation or status. Thus we may find pictures of varying degrees of comprehensibility, from easily recognised Boy Scouts to middle-aged men wearing the chains and sashes of unidentified office.

Many institutional pictures are church related. Some show social bonding activities, such as the Sunday School treat or the choir outing. Churches of all denominations were well aware of the cohesive value of communal events and activities, and in Edwardian times a camera quickly became a natural item to take on such occasions. A clerical collar might give a hint towards the placing of such activities, but if no clergyman is in attendance, or if he is behind the camera, then there may be no clue to help with accurate interpretation. Even when the associations of a picture are specific, the actual occasion may remain unclear. The Greta Carse album includes a number of pictures of Roman Catholic priests. Ages are mixed, and, though some faces appear more than once, no one figure is sufficiently in evidence for us to feel that we are following his career. Some pictures are dated on the back and are thus seen to be Edwardian or early Georgian, but no further clue is given, and whether they were taken at a seminary or retreat or some other priestly gathering is not clear. This reluctance to give up secrets is, in fact, a common feature of institutional pictures of all kinds. We may recognise no more than the general nature of a group from the image itself. There is, fortunately, a slightly better chance than normal that such pictures will have some identifying words handwritten on the back, and, with inherited photographs, there is often a possibility that family tradition will supply information that the picture itself does not give.

Education is another area for institutional photographs. Many class pictures survive, and it should be remembered that school groups need not only be of children. The second half of the nineteenth century saw the founding of various evening schools and institutes and the beginnings of adult education. Such schools, like those for children, had their group portraits and their annual tea parties.

The Greta Carse album contains an interesting selection of academic pictures. In 1909, as she came, presumably, towards the end of her teaching course at Sunderland Training College, Greta gathered together a series of postcard portraits of herself and her friends in gowns, mortar boards, smart blouses and ties, and each contributor to her collection wrote an affectionate message on the back. From nine years later, May 1919, comes a picture of Greta Carse as a teacher, presiding over her class of boys. The

Figure 31. Carte de visite; photographer unknown, (?)Dartford.

rooftops in the background suggest an unpretentious location, but the boys are smartly uniformed and Eton collared, and the injunction to sit up straight and fold their arms is obeyed with a conviction not always found in school photos.

Other institutional photos portray men in positions of importance, sometimes as civic dignitaries and sometimes as officers of a fraternal lodge. An interesting example of this kind of picture is a carte de visite, dated 6th July 1876, which takes the form of a souvenir menu for the Pattison Lodge Installation Banquet at the Royal Bull Hotel, Dartford (*see figure 31*). On the front are small portraits of Brothers Vincent, Butter and Hayes, who were to be installed. The event was to be marked by heavy eating, and the back of the carte is devoted to a menu of bewildering complexity.

Pictures relating to organisations of whatever kind commonly set the photographer the task of handling large groups. Traditionally this was, and still is, dealt with by setting up rows, one behind the other, and each at a higher level than the one in front. The row sitting on the ground, the row in chairs and the standing row are common ingredients, with possession of a chair often a symbol of rank or status. In pictures of outings the natural variation of levels found on, say, a grassy bank will, on occasion, allow more interesting and informal grouping, but in general the handling of people in numbers is predictable, whether the photograph is old or more recent.

Doing justice to a whole group and persuading all to look fetching at the same time are further problems faced by the photographer. The earlier the picture, the greater the difficulties. Even now there is always someone who blinks at the crucial moment. In the past the crucial moment was rather longer, lenses were less advanced and films or plates less responsive. A picture by Joseph Willey of the Louth Church Choir in 1867 provides a good example of the trials of the group photographer. The thirty-six strong choir is shown in front of an imposing house, of which windows, a door and stretches of wall are visible. In general, those people in the centre of the picture are in better focus than those on the outsides. This arises from the limitations of the lens. Loss of precision at the edges of an image is common, but in portraits of one or few people the edges lack a human population and short-comings tend to go unobserved. The clarity of the faces is also affected by the background against which they are seen. The men in the centre of the rear row are backed by a generally dark window area,

and their heads are well defined against it. To the right of centre, three men appear against a light section of wall; their faces assume a pale, washed-out look, and one seems almost featureless apart from hair and an area of shadow below the chin. A couple of the youngsters have failed to keep still and their faces are blurred. One of them, whom the eye picks out because he is wearing the palest jacket, is so imprecisely rendered that his head is a white amoeboid blob. Inevitably, for the presence of a joker is *de rigueur,* one boy, seated on the ground at the end of the row, is craning his head over towards the side, so that it appears to shoot out at right angles from the body. Lest these unfortunate details should be dismissed too lightly, it should be emphasised that the picture is the work of a competent professional photographer.

Public Events

Family members were sometimes participants in or spectators of events occurring beyond their circle and outside their own affiliations and interests. We may find that they took a camera with them.

Occasions involving royalty held a particular fascination. Royal portraits may turn up in albums, but there may also be records of moments when the royal world and our ancestors' world actually overlapped, and such moments, then as now, attracted photographers. The tribulations of the great in the face of the camera are not new, and on one occasion Edward VII had an importunate photographer removed by the police, when he found his emergence from Sandringham Church being treated as yet another photo-opportunity.

The early years of photography saw their share of major royal events. The 1863 wedding of the Prince of Wales and Princess Alexandra came too early for snapshots, but some pictures of celebrations and street decorations were taken and have survived. The Queen's Golden Jubilee in 1887 was also too soon for popular photography, but the Diamond Jubilee coincided with the days of the early roll film cameras. Edward VII's coronation in 1902 occurred just when the Box Brownie was opening up photography to all. Our ancestors were not generally able to record a key procession, service or ceremony, but they may have taken pictures of the decorated streets and the nation-wide celebrations that attended such events. There were, too, times when an ancestor may have been at or near the centre of the action, for royal occasions could take place on a local as well as a national level, and a family may well have obtained, by their own efforts or by buying a souvenir, a picture of a visit to their home patch. Often only an official photographer would be close enough to make the most of the opportunity, but the resulting shots could be sold and could quickly find homes in family collections throughout the area. On 5th November 1906 King Edward VII, attended by the Queen, the Prince of Wales and Princess Mary, opened the new grammar school buildings in King's Lynn and conferred a knighthood on the school's benefactor, W. J. Lancaster (*see figure 32*). A photographer was at hand and took a number of pictures which, in postcard form, found a ready market. At least four different shots survive, all taken from the same angle over a period of a minute or so. This suggests a healthy demand for mementos of the visit.

All manner of events may find their way into a family's picture archive. Some may be national. Parades and street festivities were a common way of marking major events, and there were widespread celebrations of the Relief of Mafeking in 1900 and the end of the Boer War in 1902. When trying to identify the cause of public excitement, it is worth scanning the street decorations, if necessary with a magnifying glass, since a message or motto embroidered on a banner or worked in flowers may provide the needed clue.

Other pictured occasions are purely local. These, too, often have a festive air, with May Day parades and dancing, seasonal celebrations, bands and morris men. Country fairs may have their businesslike aspect, too, with prize animals or the latest farm machinery being inspected by solemn, bowler-hatted connoisseurs. The less happy events of local life may also be depicted. The Norfolk roll film negatives include several shots of the Norwich floods of 1912, where youngsters paddle outside their houses and a horse, with cart, wades down a shopping street.

The greatest and most dreadful public event was, of course, war, and this is reflected in many albums. Though the Great War was documented in many harrowing front-line photographs, these are not to be found in the average family album. Instead, young men in uniform smile cheerily at the camera before going off to an experience the nature of which we, with hindsight, are painfully aware. Occasionally the pictures that come down to us show something of the preparation for war. A box of quarter-plate glass negatives, marked 'Territorial Camp, Worthing, & Army Manoeuvres 1913' includes, along with posed groups, pictures of field hospital wagons, tent-erection and machine-gun practice (*see figure 33*). More usual, however, is the photo of an individual or a handful of recruits. The beginnings of the war saw a boom in camera sales and a great rash of portraits of young men about to leave their families. Many albums include examples of this kind, and lucky the family whose young soldier was destined to come home and grow old. Naturally enough, families wanted pictures of those about to depart, and naturally, too, the recruits wanted pictures of their loved ones to carry with them. The result was a burst of photographic activity. Many soldiers also took cameras with them to the front line, and since this carried the risk of court-

Figure 32. Postcard; Logsdail & Co., Kings Lynn.

martial, the market for the Kodak Vest Pocket Camera flourished. This model, introduced in 1912, was what it claimed to be, and the fact that it could be slipped easily into a pocket made it very popular with the forces.

An example of the 'leaving for war' category of picture is included in the Greta Carse album. Dated 26th November 1914, the postcard shows three lance-corporals, not noticeably at ease, in front of a studio backdrop of tents (*see figure 34*). This suggests that backcloths may have been quickly prepared in the light of unfolding events, though the pictured neat camp on a pleasant site conjures up a war, time and place quite different from the trenches of reality. A later postcard, dated 26th September 1918 and French in origin, reveals that four years of war did not claim Derry Carse, who notes on the back, with traditional English sang-froid, 'The weather here is somewhat changeable.' It is hoped that he survived the few more weeks needed to bring him safely through.

There were those who returned, and they were welcomed by relieved families and a jubilant population. The signing of the Peace Treaty at the end of June 1919 was marked by street parties throughout the land. My own family collection includes a picture taken at one such celebration, showing the infant Betty Scoffin dressed as a red rose. Her cousin, also done up in crêpe-paper and sturdy boots, went as a pink rose, and their mothers were triumphantly swathed in Union Jacks. Thus the war eventually produced its happy pictures too. But between the departing youths and the street parties other events took place, the knowledge of which we cannot erase when we look at the bland pictures that have come down to us.

Figure 33. Modern print from glass negative; 'Worthing T.A.' negatives.

Dressing Up

The inclusion of dressing up in this chapter is a little arbitrary. Sometimes our ancestors dressed up in connection with an event, such as the peace celebrations, local festivities or amateur drama, but dressing up is often seen in studio photos too. Since, at any rate, it has about it a sense of special occasion, the subject is dealt with here rather than earlier.

The taste for dressing up can, at its simplest, be seen in everyday life in the desire to echo the appearance of others. Indeed, the inclination to imitation might be toyed with as an incautious definition of fashion. High on the list of those to be aped were the royal family, and their influence is seen in a number of ways. The princess line caught on in the late 1870s, continuing the full length of the body without any break or horizontal punctuation at the waist, and, like the craze for fringed hairstyles, it owed its popularity to Princess Alexandra. The Queen herself was not a great leader of fashion as far as clothes were concerned, but to her example we owe, as previously indicated, the consolidation and codification of mourning practices. It was her aroused taste, too, for all things Scottish that encouraged the profusion of tartans that we see in pictures, especially those of the young, from the 1860s on.

The Saxe-Coburgs, however, were not the only setters of imitative trends. Another group of influences were broadly literary. Exaggerated sidewhiskers may have been worn before the production of *Our American Cousin* in 1861, but it is from a character in the play, Lord Dundreary, that they received their name. Dundreary was, in fact, something of a caricature of the quasi-military heavy

Figure 34. Postcard; 'Carse' album (C. R. Stevenson collection).

swell, but satirical intent was not enough to avert the course of fashion, and dundrearies may be seen in portraits from that decade and later. From Dickens derives, by no very clear process, the Dolly Varden look. Dolly appears in *Barnaby Rudge*, which was written in the 1840s and set in 1775, and her dress is not extensively described. Yet thirty years after the novel was finished, the Dolly Varden look appeared, and photographs from the 1870s may show us the bunched-up overskirts and broad-brimmed, forward-tilted, shepherdess hats that were characteristic of it. Frances Burnett's novel, *Little Lord Fauntleroy,* condemned many small boys to wretchedness and embarrassment when it was published in the mid-eighties. The central character was an American lad inheriting an English earldom. The child was so ineffably sweet and unutterably refined that mothers everywhere went weak at the knees and dressed their sons like him, in the hope, presumably, that the clothes would confer a delicate sanctity upon their growing offspring. Thus a carte by R. S. Freeman of Notting Hill shows Duncan George Inveraity, aged seven, perched on the padded end of a sofa as the epitome of fauntleregality (*see figure 35*). He wears velvet jacket and breeches, white stockings and shiny black shoes with ankle-straps. There are bows on his upper arms, ribbons on all four limbs, lace at collar, cuffs and knees, and a brooch or medallion at his throat. Fringed fair hair cascades wavily over and beyond his shoulders. Only the cavalier hat is lacking. It is to be hoped that, beneath the innocent exterior, Duncan George is thinking healthy seven-year-old's thoughts about interesting experiments with worms.

Everyday imitation of the famous was only one expression of the taste for dressing up. There was also an enjoyment of rôle-playing. The Queen herself had some feeling for this and was depicted, at various times, simply at her spinning wheel, busily at her typewriter (with turbaned Indian attendant), and, in the part she made her own, forlornly as a widow. Before the death of her beloved consort condemned her to type-casting, Victoria showed an enjoyment of dressing up. Her children figure most frequently in the royal tableaux, but occasionally the Queen also takes part. In a group picture from 1854 Victoria and Princess Alice, simply dressed and beshawled, seem to be assuming the character of refugees, whilst three of the other children stand by showing, apparently, varying degrees of embarrassment. Costumed royal children feature in several pictures dating from the mid-fifties. The Princess Royal and Prince Arthur figure in an allegorical depiction of 'Summer', one of a series of photographs based on James Thompson's poem, 'The Seasons'. Prince Arthur appears again as a Grenadier guard, and is seen, with the Princesses Louise and Helena, in a tableau entitled 'The Allies'. In another picture those same two princesses appear as an eighteenth century footman and a country wench with ringlets, mob-cap, flower-basket, fingerless lace gloves, bows and mini-pinny. Prince Alfred seems to have been the most reluctant participant in these charades, if the picture of him sulking in long-sleeved vest, chaplet and leopard-skin is reliable evidence.

This taste for fanciful costume is also to be seen in pictures by major photographers

R.S.FREEMAN.PHOTO.   162.HICH STREET.
NOTTINC   HILL.W.

Figure 35. Carte de visite; R. S. Freeman, Notting Hill.

of the day. H. P. Robinson dressed up the daughters of his acquaintances rather than have to photograph real peasants. Julia Margaret Cameron conscripted friends, neighbours and servants for scenes based on Tennyson, and assembled groups of soulful young women got up as a sort of ambulant harvest festival. C. L. Dodgson, better known to us as Lewis Carroll, borrowed the children of his colleagues and friends for his set pieces. One of his most pleasing, because the girls are so clearly entering into the spirit of it, is a picture of six-year-old Annie Rogers and eight-year-old Mary Jackson as Queen Eleanor and Rosamund. Both are dressed up in an improvised way, with Annie wearing a cut-out crown. Eleanor looks

Figure 36. Postcard; W. Stocks, Sunderland; 'Carse' album (C. R. Stevenson collection).

stern and disapproving as she offers an abashed and unenthusiastic Rosamund the choice of dagger or poisoned chalice. Since the poisoned chalice is a mug, and since the scene smacks more of dressing-up-box than of polished theatricals, the picture has a sense of play that such photographs often lack. One of Dodgson's favourite subjects. Alice Liddell, having appeared for him as a beggar girl and in Chinese costume, fell a dozen or so years later into the clutches of the formidable Mrs Cameron, and had a whole new photo-graphic career as an angel, the Goddess of Fruitfulness and a selection of Biblical and allegorical figures. It may be that Alice Liddell is the most put-upon young person in the history of photography.

Whilst the average family album is not likely to contain the more ambitious kind of costume scene, there may be evidence of leanings in that direction, and sylvan or seascape backcloths often serve to reinforce the effect. Gipsy costume enjoyed some popularity, and rustic or British-ethnic looks found some favour. A carte by Emmett of Stalybridge, dating from the late seventies or early eighties, shows a girl with an indeterminately peasanty look. She appears dressed up rather than the genuine article, and seems to represent a tasteful and romanticised version of rustic ethnicity. A postcard in the Carse album, probably taken shortly before the First World War, shows a shepherdess against a suitably Arcadian studio backcloth (*see figure 36*). There is no doubt, however, that this is a shepherdess who never in her life touched a piece of wool that still had legs on.

Dressing up could certainly be for adults, but children were seen as its ideal subjects. This was an easy extension of the tendency to think of children as items to be displayed. As a result, quite apart from more imaginative excursions into fantasy, pictures of siblings dressed alike, of infants in tartan and of boys in sailor suits abound. Two cartes from the 1890s by Allen of Pembroke Dock typify the nautical look and are clearly intended as a matched pair. In each picture a young boy in sailor suit stands in a dinghy, the *Flora*. One boy's suit is light, the other's dark, and each has a pole in his hands, ready to push off from the shore. A seascape backdrop provides the appropriate context. The intended manly vigour of the images is reduced, however, by the comfortable furs in the boat, and by the fact that, in one picture, we can see not only the boat's name, but two flowers, perhaps included by way of explanation for the non-classical. There is thus a prettying of reality, which is a frequent feature of dressing up pictures of all kinds, where a spoonful or two of pleasant fancy is often stirred into the dramatic brew.

Bibliography

A more general bibliography for students of early photography may be found in *Dating Old Photographs*. Works in the present list have been chosen for the light they shed, sometimes incidentally, on topics considered in this book.

Briggs, Asa & Mills, Archie, *A Victorian Portrait: Victorian Life and Values as Seen Through the Works of Studio Photographers.* Cassell, 1989.

Coe, Brian & Gates, Paul, *The Snapshot Photograph – The Rise of Popular Photography, 1888-1939.* Ash & Grant, 1977.

Estabrooke, Edward M., *The Ferrotype and How to Make It.* Gatchel & Hyatt, 1872. (Reprinted in a facsimile edition by Morgan & Morgan, New York, 1972, with introduction by Eugene Ostroff.)

Ford, Colin & Steinorth, Karl, *You Press the Button – We Do the Rest. The Birth of Snapshot Photography.* Dirk Nishen in association with the National Museum of Photography, Film & Television, 1988.

Ginsburg, Madeleine, *Victorian Dress in Photographs.* Batsford, 1982.

Hiley, Michael, *Seeing Through Photographs.* Gordon Fraser, 1983.

Martin, Elizabeth, *Collecting and Preserving Old Photographs.* Collins, 1988.

Reilly, James M., *The Albumen and Salted Paper Book. (The History and Practice of Photographic Printing, 1840-1895).* Light Impressions, New York, 1980.

Richter, Stefan, *The Art of the Daguerrotype.* Viking, 1989.

Weightman, Gavin, *Pictures from the Past: The Seaside.* Collins & Brown, 1991; reprinted Selecta Books, 1993.

Of particular help in understanding the work of the professional photographer have been a number of studies of individual practitioners. (Of these, the Sutcliffe book offers fewest in the way of insights, because its written introduction is brief, but it is one of a series of books full of the pictures of a photographer for whom I confess an especial liking.)

Cuppleditch, David, *Joseph Willey – A Victorian Lincolnshire Photographer.* Charles Skilton, 1987.

Harker, Margaret F., *Henry Peach Robinson, Master of Photographic Art, 1830-1901.* Basil Blackwell, 1988.

Moffat, John S., *John Moffat of Edinburgh. A Victorian Photographer in the Family.* Genealogists' Magazine, June 1993 (Vol 24, No 6).

Shaw, Michael, (with an introduction by Bill Eglon Shaw), *Frank Meadow Sutcliffe, Photographer. A Third Selection.* The Sutcliffe Gallery, Whitby, 1990.

Taylor, Roger, *George Washington Wilson, Artist and Photographer (1823-93).* Aberdeen University Press, 1981.

General Index

Albumen prints 29, 30, 33, 34-35
Albums 30, 31, 35, 40, 47, 57-59
Ambrotypes 26, 28, 33, 42
Art and photography 12-14

Babies 25-26, 51, 52, 54, 55, 61, 66
Backcloths 10, 14, 32-3, 42, 45, 48, 56, 79
Body language of sitters 38, 40, 47-55, 56-57, 60
Box Brownie 44, 59, 69, 73
Burnett, Francis 76

Cabinet prints 4, 27, 30, 33, 40, 41, 42, 49, 55, 56, 57, 58, 68
Calotypes 41
Card mounts 12-15, 72
'Carse' album 65-66, 69, 71, 74, 78, 79
Cartes de visite 8, 9, 11, 19, 20, 21, 23, 24, 25, 26, 27, 29, 30, 39, 42, 44, 45, 46, 48, 49, 50, 51, 52, 53, 54, 55, 56, 57, 58, 71, 76, 77, 79
'Character' 44-47
Chemicals 11, 15-16, 22
Children 23-26, 50-55, 56, 64, 71, 76, 77, 78, 79
Christenings 66
Church activities 70
Civic status of photographers 15
Class 35, 41-44, 63-64, 65-66
Clergymen 19, 45-46, 59, 69, 71
Clothing suggested by photographers 7, 16-17, 23, 32
Colour representation 16, 31-33, 43, 57

Contrasts 55-56
Couples 47-50

Daguerrotypes 7, 9, 26, 28, 33, 41
Death 67-69
Deterioration 28-30
Dickens, Charles 63, 76
Doorways 45, 61
Dressing up 75-79
Dry plate photography 20-21
Dundrearies 57, 75-76

Eastlake, Lady 5
Education 71
Emigrants 35, 47
Exposure times 7, 20, 21, 22, 23, 31-32, 60

Fading 29
Family 44, 47-55, 66-68
Fashion, aspects of 32, 40, 43, 53, 55, 57, 58-59, 60, 64, 65, 75-77, 79
Fauntleroy, Little Lord 76-77
Ferrotypes (tintypes) 8, 27, 28-29, 33, 35
Flyleaves 30-31
Focus 18, 20, 61, 72
Forceps, photographics 31
Foxing 29
'Freddie' album 30, 60, 61, 65
Furniture, studio 10, 42, 45, 46

Gardens 60, 61-62
Gelatine 29, 30

Glass negatives 29, 73, 75
Group photographs 18, 72

Head rests 19-20, 23, 46, 53
Health of photographers 15-16
Holidays 43-44, 63-66
Houses 61-62

Identification of sitters 57-58, 59
Institutional pictures 70-72

Kodak 9, 62, 74

Liddell, Alice 78
Lighting 7, 8, 9-10, 21

Mayhew, Henry 7
Monograms 15
Mounts, card 12-15
Mourning 67, 75
Munby, A. J. 22-23, 43

Nature and photography 14, 57
'Norfolk' roll film negatives 60, 64,
    69, 73

Outings 43-44, 60, 66

Parents 50-53
Patrons, distinguished 14-15
Personality of sitter 38-40
Pliny 6
Posing 17-19
Postcards 48, 65, 66, 71, 73, 74, 78, 79
Prices 7, 8, 26-27, 33, 57
Processing 11, 12, 29, 36-37

Props 23-25, 39, 40, 45, 79
Public events 72-74

Queen Victoria 5, 14, 15, 26, 45, 48-49, 58,
    65, 67, 68, 75, 77

Retouching 34
Rôles, family 25, 47-55, 56, 60
Rôles, gender 25, 40, 45-46, 47-50, 51,
    54, 55, 56-57, 60
Rôles, social 38, 42-43, 45
Roll film photography 29, 30, 36-37, 39,
    40, 44, 59-62, 63, 64, 65, 69
Royalty (other than Victoria) 14-15, 64,
    67, 72-73, 75, 77

Seaside photographs 25, 63-65, 79
Smiles, Samuel 44
Snapshot photography 59-62
Soldiers 48, 69, 73-74
Sport 69-70
Stereotyping 24, 56-57
Studios 8-12

Tension in sitters 19, 22, 38, 39, 45, 52
Tinting 27, 33
Tintypes (ferrotypes) 8, 27, 28-29,
    33, 35
Toys 23-25
Trollope, Anthony 38

Vanity 19
Vest pocket camera 74
Victoria, Queen 5, 14, 15, 26, 45, 48-49,
    58, 65, 67, 68, 75, 77
Vignettes 17, 29, 36-37, 58

War 73-74

Weddings 67

Wet plate photography 11-12, 20, 38

Women photographers 7, 12, 62

Women workers in photography 11, 12

Work 69

Working women 22, 43, 58-59

'Worthing T. A.' negatives 73, 75

Index of Photographers and Photographic Suppliers

Adamson, Robert 41, 42
Allen (of Pembroke Dock) 79
Audas, W. 15

Bailey, A. J. 4, 12, 13, 15, 49
Banks, R. 12, 14
Bardsley, Mrs J. 12
Beales, F. 15
Beard, Richard 7, 16, 17, 26
Bertolle, R. F. 51
Bingen, Maiben and 67
Bliss, J. E. 26, 27
Boak (of Bridlington) 8
Bowman, James 53
Boxell, Thomas 15
Bradshaw, J. C. 56
Brady, Matthew 9
Brooks, David 12
Brunton, W. 52, 53

Cade, R. 14
Cameron, Julia Margaret 62, 77, 78
Carroll, Lewis (C. L. Dodgson) 78
Claudet, Antoine 7, 10
Cole, F. 13
Cromack (of Scarborough) 68
Currey (of Bolton & Morecambe) 14

Dickinson, C. T. Y. 15
Disderi, André Adolphe 42
Dodgson, C. L. (Lewis Carroll) 78
Douglas, J. 45, 46
Downey, W. and D. 18, 19, 45

Eastman, George 9, 62
Emerson, P. H. 32, 42
Emmett, W. 30, 44, 79
Estabrkoke, Edward M. 10, 17, 18, 23, 35

Fannin, Watson and 26
Faulkner, Edwin 14
Fenton, Roger 67
Freeman, R.S. 15, 76, 77
Fry, A.H. 9

Gatchel and Hyatt 10
Glanville, George 23, 24
Gotto, Parkins and 57
Gregson (of Halifax and Bristol) 49

Hall and Son 57
Hamel, Monsieur H. J. M. 51
Hammond, R. 13
Hampton (of Glasgow) 12, 15, 30
Harrison, F. S. 50, 55
Hawarden, Clementina, Lady 62
Hawke, John 14, 18
Hay and Wilson 27, 33
Hellis and Son 14, 42
Hopson, George 14
Huther, M. 54
Hyatt, Gatchel and 27

James, Arthur 27
Jeanes, J. 12

Kay, John 11
Keig, T 12, 40, 41
Kennerell, J. 49

King, James 46

Lamb, John 26
Logsdail and Co. 74
London and Chester Photographic
    Company 8
London Photographic Company 26, 27
London Portrait Company 15
Luck, Walter 54
Lund (of Photographic Forceps) 31

Maclean, J. 56
Maiben and Bingham 67
Maltby, W. F. 12
Mayall, John E. 7, 16, 42
Messer, Walter 15
Miller, F. W. 13
Mizon, Charles 14
Moffatt, John 9, 19, 22
Moss, Mrs. E. 12

O'Shea, H. 12

Palmer, Frederick C. 31, 55, 58
Parkins and Gotto 57
Phillips, W. M. 13
Plumbe, John 22

Reston (of Stretford) 12
Rodrigues (of Picadilly) 57
Robinson, Henry Peach 15, 16, 18, 19, 21,
    23, 26, 27, 34, 37, 42, 77
Robinson, M. 12
Robinson, Mrs 12

Sauvy, Monsier 12
Sawyer's Italian Studios 20
Scott, Charles Stuart 49
Shaw, J. E. 57
Silvy, Camille 42
Sing, Hop, and Co. 3
Smith and Sons 14, 15
Southwell Brothers 14
Spencer, E. D. 13
Stocks, W. 78
Sutcliffe, Frank Meadow 21, 25-26, 42, 55

Talbot, William Henry Fox 5, 14, 41
Taylor, A. and G. 14, 42
Thomas, J. W. 13
Thompson, C. J. 52
Thompson, L. W. 56
Turnbull and Sons 40

Vieler, Emil 14

Walton, F. 22, 23, 52
Walton (of Leeds and Manchester) 27
Waterfield, W. H. 21, 39, 54
Watson and Fannin 26
White, John 15, 24, 25, 54, 55
Willey, Joseph 10, 26, 39, 52, 54, 72
Willson, R. Roberts 48
Wilson, George Washington 15, 16, 17,
    18, 21, 22, 26, 27, 28, 33
Wright, R. 26, 51
Wright, T. 12
Wyatt, Dr. Andrew 16